To Arch...
keep to...
minter Wh...

I Was In Prison

Archibald,
God bless
you for your
ministry among
enmates!
Mark Hick

Archibald—
Bless you!
Patricia Barrett

I Was In Prison

United Methodist Perspectives on Prison Ministry

EDITED BY
James M. Shopshire, Sr.; Mark C. Hicks;
and Richmond Stoglin

General Board of Higher Education and Ministry
The United Methodist Church
Nashville, Tennessee

The General Board of Higher Education and Ministry leads and serves The United Methodist Church in the recruitment, preparation, nurture, education, and support of Christian leaders—lay and clergy—for the work of making disciples of Jesus Christ for the transformation of the world. Its vision is that a new generation of Christian leaders will commit boldly to Jesus Christ and be characterized by intellectual excellence, moral integrity, spiritual courage, and holiness of heart and life.

The General Board of Higher Education and Ministry of The United Methodist Church is the church's agency for educational, institutional, and ministerial leadership. It serves as an advocate for the intellectual life of the church. The Board's mission embodies the Wesleyan tradition of commitment to the education of laypersons and ordained persons by providing access to higher education for all persons.

ISBN 978-0-938162-89-6

Produced by the Office of Interpretation

Manufactured in the United States of America

For Pat Barrett,
faithful friend, passionate advocate, and dedicated colleague in ministry
with those on the inside and those on the outside

CONTENTS

CONTENTS

FOREWORD

GREGORY VAUGHN PALMER

I am honored and humbled to have been asked to offer the foreword to *I Was In Prison: United Methodist Perspectives on Prison Ministry*. The General Board of Higher Education and Ministry is greatly wise in commissioning this volume. The editors and authors have given the church a great gift in this book that passionately, knowledgeably, and skillfully calls the church to see and to pay attention to what and whom we might otherwise be more comfortable in ignoring.

In the main, church leaders (including, if not especially, bishops) and churches have lost sight of our vocation to engage those who are in prison, the victims of their crimes, and the laws, policies, and practices of the criminal justice system. As I read through this book, I thought this piece was both long overdue and yet right on time. It is long overdue in the sense that there is far too much material available to us church folk about how to be more appealing so we can get people who are just like us inside our doors. But it is right on time because, as a church both obsessive and compulsive about our decline and anxious about our institutional future, *I Was In Prison* calls us afresh to regain our souls by going where the hurt is and casting our lot with the most vulnerable.

This book did not make me feel good about myself and the practice of my discipleship and ministry. For that matter, after reading it, I did not feel all that great about the church. My—and our—derelictions and delinquencies have been exposed and laid utterly bare. But feeling good is not what this book is about. Its aim, in my judgment, is to awaken the church called United Methodist to the gospel and to our Wesleyan roots. And while, on first blush, in reading these pages you too might not feel good, you will find yourself hopeful that we can be different as a church and, in so being, do differently.

The authors adroitly provide us with helpful and needed biblical, theological, sociological, and ecclesial background. The paths they lead us down are generously supported with careful documentation and a roadmap for further delving into prison ministry and restorative justice. This background assists us in seeing more clearly. But, when all is said and done, the authors and editors warn us, where we really lack is not in finding words, statistics, and information. Where we lack is in the doing. I invite you to join me in this doing.

The mission of The United Methodist Church is "to make disciples of Jesus Christ for the transformation of the world" (*Book of Discipline—2008*, ¶120). I boldly suggest that the current volume will assist us in being conformed to this mission. And in the process we might just be made true disciples who join God in the transformation of the world that God loves so much.

INTRODUCTION

JAMES M. SHOPSHIRE, SR.; MARK C. HICKS; AND RICHMOND STOGLIN

In the early part of the twenty-first century, we find ourselves confronted with complex issues in the criminal justice system of the
United States. While not limited to this country, criminal justice is
a crucial concern for both church and society as justice, peace, order,
and dignity become more difficult to achieve in the massive community of humankind. Both ideology and policy are located at the heart
of a struggle to define and implement a just system to deal with
destructive criminal behaviors. The churches, no strangers to participating in and influencing public policy, are called to bring faithful
responses to the task of criminal justice. All churches, The United
Methodist Church in particular, are located in the midst of and are
challenged by this quest to develop just and sustainable practices for
the present and the future. Such practices go beyond simply punishment and retribution. In the most basic sense, if the quest for personal and social holiness does not take into account a holistic
meaning of God's mission and work to restore humanity to righteous
relationship, then the church will have missed the mark of its high
calling to be the people of God. Unless the ministry of the churches
can deliver the message and work of restorative caring to individuals
and groups—to the private, communal, and public places and

processes of our lives—then our responsive ministry cannot be the instrument of God's grace in this world.

The problem of crime and justice manifests itself in many parts of the globe and raises difficult questions. How can we sanction and correct those who break the rules (laws), as well as restore those who are broken by criminal actions? How can we as people of faith participate in activities intended to provide social order, peace, and justice, both at home and in societies all over the world (which we United Methodists cite as our "parish")?

Criminal Injustice and the Promise of Restorative Justice

In the continuing quest for freedom, equality, and justice in the nation and the criminal justice system, the approach of restorative justice taken in this book offers a comprehensive means of restoring lives to vitality. It is an approach that moves beyond simply administering punishment to healing and renewal of meaningful relationships for people and communities. Restorative justice advocates and facilitates interaction between victim and offender that aims for cooperative resolution of harm and making amends for criminal behavior. As a functional paradigm, it promotes responsible action to make right what is wrong and rebuild relationships in community and society. Restorative justice moves away from adversarial and retributive remedies that rely too heavily on warehousing large numbers of human beings. Instead, cooperation and mediation hold out greater promise for dealing with crime.

Restoration of relationships and reconciliation of the wounded with the perpetrator is a model that the Christian church should readily comprehend and embrace. The primary story of the church is about God, who acts to redeem humanity and bring people back to right relationship and responsible behavior. In that light, restorative justice is a central theme of this book. The concept affords a "sacred canopy" under which the many facets of prison ministry and criminal justice ministry may be addressed from a holistic perspective. Although the approaches in the chapters that follow may vary, the theme of restoration is lifted up as theologically salient and promising for the work of sanctifying grace. Restorative justice commends itself as an appropriate paradigm for the proactive criminal justice ministry of The United Methodist Church.

Over the years, considerable criminal injustice has emerged in the gap between the poor and the wealthy and between people of color and "White" ethnics across the globe. Poverty and destructive racial-ethnic and gender relations—all combined to raise questions of equality and dignity for humankind. The buying and selling of Black humanity like commodities on the market during American slavery represented a form of incarceration in a system of abominable injustice that violated the dignity of many people. We have yet to accomplish proper correction or restoration of criminals and victims for the crimes of the past five hundred years. To this day, many longstanding injustices continue to disproportionately impact people of color and to negatively influence our patterns of social relating.

Criminal justice is always about what is righteous and good in terms of our most sacred meanings and values. Even if one accepts the questionable argument that what is past is past and should be forgotten, there is no escape from the need to learn and live out truly reconciling and restorative patterns of relating. Such patterns encompass all of life—from the depths of a criminal past to the struggle for justice in the here and now.

In contemporary processes of criminal justice, the most neglected persons in the legal system are those who are offended, traumatized, and wounded. Although many, if not most, survive assault by criminals, they are often left traumatized, with little opportunity for the healing and restoration of the broken places in their lives. It is unconscionable that people who lose their health, their limbs, their hard-earned resources, and their relationships with loved ones often have the least to show after the criminal justice system finishes their case. As a result of crimes perpetrated against them, persons, families, neighborhoods, organizations, and whole communities often are bereft of life, joyful relationships, and resources.

Although the wider scope of the challenge is global, the pressures that test us most immediately in criminal and restorative justice are in the United States. This country should give leadership and compass to the world in a number of aspects of living and relating. Yet the sad fact is that, in the policy and practice of criminal justice, the United States lags far behind many more forward-looking nations. The number of people incarcerated in our federal, state, county, and local prisons and jails is a primary indicator of our relative ineffectiveness. Many of the 2.3 million people incarcerated in the United States face sentences that hardly seem to fit the crimes. Many others have been summarily sentenced to longer periods than others who committed similar offenses. The record shows that many have received long, harsh sentences for nonviolent, relatively minor drug-related offences. These facts raise serious questions about who receives what they justly deserve and whether what is called justice is truly just.[1]

To make matters worse, physical incarceration in prisons and jails has become tied to the greedy quest of making economic profit at any cost, thereby involving legal mechanisms that trample essential values located in both the biblical and traditional heritage of the church and the founding principles and ideals of the United States of America. The rarely exposed "prison-industrial complex" illustrates the point well. The book The Celling of America includes a careful look at look at the prison-industrial complex in the United States.[2]

United Methodists and Prison Ministry: Approach and Scope of the Book

Looking in retrospect, prison ministry in the United States of America has proceeded in fits and starts. The predecessor bodies of The United Methodist Church share a close historical connection with the nation, the United States. The Methodist Episcopal Church and this country were formally organized during the same period. Both the church and the nation struggled mightily with the fundamental questions regarding the value and sanctity of life for all humankind. Both failed measurably in living out the values of the Christian and Wesleyan heritage and the founding principles of the nation. And now, some 232 years later, both continue to struggle with issues pertaining to crime and criminal justice within the larger realm of the rights and dignity of humankind and justice in the land.

The rich heritage of prison ministry that began with the Wesleys remains as a standard for United Methodist reflection and action in our time. The Wesleyan heritage challenges and informs both church and nation anew about the matters of criminal justice and incarceration. Today, through various aspects of the connectional system, The United Methodist Church endeavors to promote reform in prison policy and to support movement toward faithful ministries of restorative justice. The ebb and flow of these efforts can be seen in the work for justice in keeping with our biblical heritage. The work continues in John and Charles Wesley's guidelines for social holiness to the original Social Creed (1908) to the current Social Principles and Social Creed.[3] In the final analysis, the bedrock values that flow from God's agape love-justice to all humanity are undeniable. For United Methodists, the basic human rights to freedom, justice, equality, and dignity are, first and foremost, sacred values.

The connectional system is the primary means by which prison ministry and restorative justice are pursued in The United Methodist Church. Serving effectively, more or less, through what they do, many such ministries have a limited view of the scope of prison ministry. Some efforts extract from the biblical witness the requirement to visit the prisoner—a simple ministry of presence. Others hear in the call the responsibility to teach, preach, and minister to the sometimes broken and misguided and to those who are unrepentant and uncaring about their offences. Still others embrace a larger and more comprehensive approach to be agents of restoration helping formerly incarcerated people to reenter community with healthy life possibilities with their families, and doing the same for the victims of criminal behaviors and their families. Finally, ministers and agencies of the church variously seek to participate in criminal justice and prison-related ministries by addressing questions of policy among the systems and structures designed to administer criminal justice and benefit community and society. All of these persons, groups, structures, and institutions are important in the scope of prison ministry in the criminal justice system.

Yet there remains an urgent need for a comprehensive, holistic approach to prison ministry in The United Methodist Church today. A new paradigm would work to integrate the various aspects of ministry mentioned above around a common commitment to restorative justice. This book offers the rudiments of such a holistic approach and, in it various chapters, a detailed discussion of key aspects and important actors in the ministry.

Consequently, this book takes a holistic approach to The United Methodist Church's ministry with the incarcerated, and with people in congregations and communities. To be effective, this ministry must be pursued with the "care-full" involvement of the people of God—those reclaimed, justified, and sanctified—and those who are responsible for the administration of various parts of the criminal justice system. That is to say, the denomination's overarching prison, criminal justice and restorative justice ministry should encompass aspects of personal and pastoral caring, prophetic proclamation, and proactive response in service and commitment to policy reform for individuals, families, communities, and the larger society. The whole extended pattern of relationships in prison ministry should be embraced and acted upon as an integral part of the church's ministry within the wider scope of what God is doing in mission to the world.

In The United Methodist Church are three primary but overlapping ministry groups or communities organized to deal with different aspects of criminal justice ministry. (1) Endorsed chaplains and other ministers who serve primarily inside prisons: The chaplains focus on counseling incarcerated persons and, in some situations, religious advisors and worship leaders within prisons and jails. (2) Congregational and community-based ministers and ministries who, with direct access to persons on the inside, assist with worship, religious study, and teaching: These ministers are what we call "outside/inside" practitioners. Many of those who minister to incarcerated persons through scheduled visits on the inside also relate to families on the outside, assist with keeping families related to prisoners, engage in advocacy ministries, and help persons reenter the wider community. Most of the ministers on the outside meet the basic requirements for ministry of clergy and laypersons in The United Methodist

Church without the special preparation for endorsement to prison chaplaincy. (3) Seminaries and theological schools: This community is primarily concerned with equipping persons for ministry as chaplains, pastors of local churches, and community-based ministries inside and outside the prison walls. United Methodist seminaries have a mixed record of productive participation in preparing persons for general and specialized ministries. Yet there are many possibilities for strong contributions by the church's academies.

The chapters in this book engage these three communities (and several variations on them) in various ways, at several levels, and in different contexts. And, appropriately, the authors bring varying perspectives on and approaches to prison ministry. Yet a shared concern with restorative justice, grounded in Scripture, tradition, and current United Methodist ministries, weaves a common thread throughout.

The aim in gathering this compendium of perspectives is to engage a wide range of United Methodist leaders, both clergy and lay, in conversation about a set of urgent questions related to the work of criminal justice and prison ministry: How can United Methodists respond with integrity to the work of criminal justice and prison ministry in the United States today? How do we join, support, and empower those who seek to do justice in systems intended to correct what is wrong and restore to wholeness what has been broken? And when and how do we challenge, critique—even resist—compelled by our vision of God's love and justice and our calling as God's people?

In the pages that follow, the authors, drawing on rich and diverse experience with the three principal ministry communities involved in United Methodist criminal justice and prison ministry, address the theological, sociological, biblical, institutional, and practical dimensions of these and related questions. The two chapters in Section 1 introduce the key concept of restorative justice as well as the three ministry communities that are central to United Methodist engagement with criminal justice and prison ministry. In these chapters, James M. Shopshire, Sr.; Richmond Stoglin; and Mark C. Hicks provide a socio-theological perspective on restorative justice and outline its importance for United Methodist engagement with criminal justice and prison ministry. They define crucial relationships; raise key issues concerning the convergence of religious and other worldviews around the notions of restorative justice, criminal justice, and prison ministry; and tell the story of the three ministry communities identified above. This section articulates the general outlook relative to prison ministry compiled from the Criminal Justice Summit, convened in 2005 under the auspices of the United Methodist General Board of Higher Education and Ministry.

Section 2 examines the sociological and biblical-theological dimensions of prison ministry. In Chapter 3, James Shopshire, Sr., takes stock of the ways in which religious worldviews and secular meaning systems converge around the restorative ideal. He traces the "socio-logic" of justice ministry to, with, for, and, occasionally, against the systems intended to mete out justice in society. A socio-logic for justice ministry is based on the premise that the God of love and justice is weary of sentimental talk about justice-in-general and is pulling us into action in light of what is lacking in the work of restorative justice in social community. Josiah U. Young moves to a biblical-theological assessment of restorative justice in Chapter 4. Drawing on the rich resources of Scripture and theology, Young outlines the foundations for a holistic approach to prison ministry that can help United Methodists engage with integrity in diverse personal and social ministries with the incarcerated.

The two chapters in Section 3 provide a historical overview and interpretation of prison ministry in the early stages of Methodism in England and over the last generation of prison ministry through The United Methodist Church in the United States. In Chapter 5, Richard Heitzenrater provides a fascinating portrait of early Methodists' work with the incarcerated in eighteenth-century England. Drawing on the theology, preaching, hymnody, and ministerial practice of Methodism's founders, John and Charles Wesley, Heitzenrater shows that social reform of prisons, ministries with incarcerated persons, and pursuit of just relationships with the poor were bedrock values of the early Methodist movement—and can be for United Methodists today also.

In Chapter 6, Patricia Barrett describes her journey in prison ministry, beginning with early exposure to jails in 1970 as a seminarian, continuing to service in state correctional facilities, and concluding with her present service at the General Board of Higher Education and Ministry as the denomination's endorsing agent. In chronicling her story, Barrett simultaneously offers glimpses into the recent history of United Methodist prison ministry as well as highlights key challenges facing a vibrant prison ministry in the future.

Section 4 turns to issues emerging in the practice of ministry with those in prison, with their families, and loved ones, and with prisoners who have been released back into society. Chapter 7, by Janet Wolf, explores the many faces in/of prisons and the needs, problems, issues, and methods used for healing and restoring persons to wholesome life. Then, using the tools of pastoral care and counseling as a lens, Wolf examines matters pertaining to victims and offenders, officials of the criminal justice system, and issues of gender, sexuality, age, race, and ethnicity. In Chapter 8, Dallas Terrell addresses the difficult issue of reentry of ex-offenders into society—the restoration of prisoners to the persons, primary groups, and communities outside the walls that await and sometimes fear their return. One of the questions facing The United Methodist Church is how a socio-theology of restorative justice may work to extend ministry to families on the outside and ex-offenders reentering home and community.

The concluding chapter, Chapter 9, is also the culmination of the book. Here editors Shopshire, Stoglin, and Hicks engage the question: "What can—indeed, what *should*—the people called United Methodists do to enable, nurture, and support faithful and effective prison ministries, with a clear understanding of their meaning and importance for restorative justice?" In responding to this question, the authors draw on insights from the 2005 Criminal Justice Summit, in which the three ministry communities discussed in these pages featured prominently both in presence and in leadership. For Shopshire, Stoglin, and Hicks, the partnership between these three ministry communities, along with other congregational, annual conference, and general church agency resources comprise the leadership framework needed for vital restorative ministry in The United Methodist Church in the twenty-first century.

NOTES

1. Marc Mauer, *Race to Incarcerate*, revised and updated (New York: The New Press, 2006), 30–35. Published by The Sentencing Project, this book provides one of the most penetrating interpretations of Bureau of Justice Statistics reports concerning disparities in incarceration outcomes. The rapid rate of increase for nonviolent and drug offences over the past twenty-five years is startling. Another report by The Sentencing Project—"A 25-Year Quagmire: The War on Drugs and Its Impact on American Society," by Marc Mauer and Ryan S. King (September 2007, 1–2)—confirms that the rapid rate of increase in incarceration for nonviolent crimes continues in the United States. The full report is available online at *www.thesentencingproject.org.*

2. Daniel Burton-Rose, ed., with Dan Pens and Paul Wright, *The Celling of America: An Inside Look at the U.S. Prison Industry* (Monroe, ME: Common Courage Press, 1998).

3. See *The Book of Discipline of The United Methodist Church—2008* (Nashville: The United Methodist Publishing House, 2008), 97–131.

Section 1

Restorative Justice and Ministry

CHAPTER 1

Restorative Justice: Foundation for Prison Ministry and Criminal Justice

JAMES M. SHOPSHIRE, SR.; MARK C. HICKS; AND RICHMOND STOGLIN

Restorative Justice in Common Culture

For many people on the street and in the congregation, the idea of restorative justice presents a problem. They wonder if it is just shorthand for "coddling criminals." Some people fear that socially unacceptable behaviors may simply be overlooked or excused; others worry that people who commit terrible crimes will use the concept to get out of jail without paying the price for criminal acts.

This book, and this chapter, brooks no such simple escape from responsibility and accountability. Socially responsible attitudes and policies should take into account the need to restrain inappropriate conduct among individual and corporate entities. Any adequate social covenant must address the need for safety in the context of community; institutionalize the requirement for accountability; and encourage constructive participation by individuals and groups in

3

restitution for harm done and restoration of personal, interpersonal, and social relationships. Therefore, we go to great lengths to reinterpret and illustrate how the concept of restorative justice is both a personal and social construct for just and peaceful relationships. Restorative justice is ideological and theological, with roots in our religious heritage and our civil historical legacy. Restorative justice is a strong paradigm for interpreting how righteous, caring, and redemptive relationships can be fostered for the good of all who seek happiness, fulfillment of justice, and restoration of personal and social wholeness.

In 2005, the General Board of Higher Education and Ministry sponsored a Criminal Justice Summit to revisit in what ways and how United Methodists should respond to the needs in prison ministry and the crisis in criminal justice. It is our belief that United Methodists can appropriate and employ a restorative justice paradigm to find creative, responsible, faithful, and effective ways to respond in church and society. In what follows, we outline key biblical, theological, and practical components of such a paradigm.

The Theo-Ethical Basis of Restorative Justice

The concept of restorative justice is difficult to define. It is even more difficult to find agreement about its conceptual and operational meaning. Yet, for this rich concept to inform United Methodist thinking about prison ministry, we must risk an interpretation, however tentative. To begin, consider the word *restorative*. The root verb, *restore*, can mean "to put back into order." To restore is to recover, to bring together what has been scattered or separated, to redeem from a lesser condition, to reconstruct something that has been broken, to rebuild what has been destroyed or dismantled. For a social context to restore itself means to initiate a creative and constructive process that brings together the parts into a whole. When a person or community loses its unifying purpose and relationship, a process is needed that would bring it back together, that would "re-order" its relationships.

Disorder and broken relationships can come from several sources. Sometimes a simple misunderstanding or a lack of true understanding can rupture a relationship. Sometimes enlarged egos or unbridled greed can result in brokenness. At other times, willful violation of the laws of the social contract or covenant fractures the right relationship with God, between individuals, and within groups. Yet, because we believe in a God who is the creative restorer of relationship, we commit ourselves to processes of restorative action in ministry with the incarcerated.

The word *justice* has been variously defined—theologically, ideologically, legally, and morally (with considerable overlap between the last two). The term *justice* can be analytically partitioned in terms of the personal and social implications as borne out in various aspects of social life with implications for economic, political, and cultural relations and outcomes.

About twenty years ago, attention to the growing racial disparities in criminal justice in the United States became more focused, highlighting the need for fresh thinking about the meaning of justice, especially in the church. The book *Black Men in Prison: The Response of the African American Church*, edited by Gayraud Wilmore, broached just such new perspectives. In that volume, Henry C. Gregory, III, refers to five forms of justice in the New Testament, identified by Cain Hope Felder: reciprocal, eschatological, compensatory, commutative, and charismatic-distributive. Biblical teaching, according to Felder, supports the idea that justice is fundamentally for the creation and maintenance of wholesome human community. The biblical vision undergirds the claims that crime causes injury to another person; that law reinforces values and shows how values can be demonstrated; and that the criminal justice system must restore the victim, hold the offender responsible, and promote reconciliation between the two in order to facilitate reintegration of both into the life of the community.[1]

James Bruckner notes two meanings of *justice* in Hebrew. One is "justice-judgment" from the law, a strict form of justice in which each person receives his or her due. Justice-judgment, says Bruckner, "is grounded in a formal equilibrium of rewarding good behavior and judging law breakers. God's goal in justice-judgment is not simply equilibrium, but restoration. To that end, it involves repentance.

God's transforming grace, mercy and blessing are intended to flow from this kind of judging-justice." The second meaning of justice is "justice-righteousness." This form of justice goes beyond strict justice, implying not "soft justice" but justice done with kindness and generosity. Justice-righteousness means "intelligent, loving reflection, and action that restores health and well-being to communities and individuals. It is often used with the words 'rescue,' 'defend,' 'plead,' and 'deliver.'[2] *Justice* thus defined opens the door and points the way to making "the uneven ground . . . level and the rough places a plain" (Isa. 40:4) in the patterned relationships of persons and societies.

Even this brief overview of the various meanings of restorative justice allows us to anticipate several insights that will reverberate throughout the chapters in this book. First, Scripture supports a restorative vision of justice. Second, justice is both personal and communal. Third, restorative justice finds expression in a variety of definitions and forms in the larger society. Fourth, restorative justice connects well with the emphasis on sanctifying grace, in both its personal and social dimensions, at the heart of our Wesleyan heritage. We are persuaded that restorative justice can be the orienting symbol for a powerful paradigm of United Methodist prison ministry—an approach to our work with the incarcerated that not only allows clear-eyed assessment of our current ministry but also opens new ways to engage the criminal justice system with theological and missional integrity.

More and more resources for reflecting on our ministry in the criminal justice system are now available to the church and the community. The United Methodist *Book of Resolutions* offers strong support for restorative justice, rather than retributive justice approaches, based on solid biblical and theological argument. The resolution "Mission Plan for Restorative Justice Ministries" outlines an approach to restorative justice ministries in which justice is affirmed as a basic principle in God's creative and redemptive work for wholesome life and relationships. God sets us in the midst of the world community, the national community, and the local community to extend the work of healing, peacemaking, and reconciliation in the face of "brokenness, violence, and vengeance."[3]

A vision of restorative justice for United Methodists embraces the call for all Christians to be "healers, peacemakers and reconcilers"[4]; that is, restorers of the fractures of our lives and our times. Victims, offenders, and the community receive the ministrations of healing and transforming ministry. The faith community is challenged to lead the way in restorative justice. The resolution continues:

> The church must initiate models of restorative justice with service providers, policy makers, and law enforcement. We need to work in partnership with the criminal justice system to make it more open, accessible, humane, effective, rehabilitative, and less costly. We need to see our own capacity in community breakdowns and in the racism and classism present in the enactment and enforcement of criminal law. We must also advocate for social and economic justice to see the restoration and strengthening of our communities.[5]

Restorative Justice: The Contemporary Movement in Church and Society

Both church and nation need critically to assess our responsibility for social justice—justice that renews, reconciles, and restores people to productive relationships in families, churches, and communities. Although deeply rooted in the biblical dynamic of saving grace, the idea of restorative justice in processes of meting out criminal justice draws heavily on the current movement for restorative justice. In this context, restorative justice pursues a holistic approach in dealing with crime by advocating for a cooperative process that involves all the parties—offenders, victims, and communities. The Centre for Justice and Reconciliation, the justice reform section of Prison Fellowship International, outlines a number of principles, practices, processes, and programs that aim to restore relationships within and between persons and communities. The following practices are widely advocated:

1. Identifying and taking steps to repair harm;
2. Involving all stakeholders; and

3. Transforming the traditional relationship between communities and their governments in responding to crime.

Restorative justice programs have been developed to variously involve victim–offender mediation, conferencing, circles, victim assistance, ex-offender assistance, restitution, and community service.[6]

The Centre for Justice and Reconciliation is a prominent advocacy group for restorative justice. There are many others, including the Victim-Offender Reconciliation Program (VORP), Prison Fellowship International, and Restorative Justice Online (a service of the Centre for Justice and Reconciliation).[7]

The restorative justice movement operates on these basic principles:

1. Justice requires that we work to restore those who have been injured.
2. Those most directly involved and affected by crime should have the opportunity to participate fully in the response if they wish.
3. Government's role is to preserve a just public order and the community's role is to build and maintain a just peace.

These principles find expression in four values that lead to a set of processes for practicing restorative justice:

1. Encounter: Create opportunities for victim, offender, and community members to meet to discuss the crime and its aftermath.
2. Amends: Expect offenders to take steps to repair the harm they have caused.
3. Reintegration: Seek to restore victims and offenders to whole, contributing members of society.
4. Inclusion: Provide opportunities for parties with a stake in a specific crime to participate in its resolution.[8]

Restorative Justice: Challenge to United Methodists

What roles might The United Methodist Church or United Methodist congregations play in restorative justice? Is harsh punishment for crime the only drummer to which the churches must march? Must all of the ministries of the churches be after the fact and involve only religious services to warehoused offenders and embittered victims? Is "getting tougher on crime and criminals" an effective means of restoring justice? Would an emphasis on restitution, instead of retribution, be more conducive to restoration?

In varying ways, on several levels, and in addressing different ministry communities, the authors in this book respond to these questions and explore a range of possibilities through which the ministries of the church can faithfully and responsibly touch base with the work of restorative justice through prison ministry. The added impetus may well increase the support in the church for theologically sound approaches to ministry with the incarcerated.

NOTES

1. Henry C. Gregory, III, "Incarceration and Rehabilitation: A Challenge to the African Church and Academy," in *Black Men in Prison: The Response of the African American Church*, ed. Gayraud Wilmore (Atlanta: Interdenominational Center Press, 1990), 17–19.

2. James K. Bruckner. "Justice in Scripture," *Ex Auditu* 22 (2006):1. Used by permission. Online at *http://www.wipfandstock.com*.

3. "Mission Plan for Restorative Justice Ministries," *The Book of Resolutions of The United Methodist Church—2008* (Nashville: The United Methodist Publishing House, 2008), 673.

4. Ibid.

5. Ibid., 677.

6. See "Centre for Justice and Reconciliation," sponsored by Prison Fellowship International; online at *http://www.pficjr.org/programs*.

7. Information on these programs is available online: Victim–Offender Reconciliation Program (*http://www.vorp.com*); Prison Fellowship International (*http://www.pfi.org*); Restorative Justice Online (*http://www.restorativejustice.org*).

8. For more information on these principles and values, visit Restorative Justice Online (*http://www.restorativejustice.org/intro*).

CHAPTER 2

The Three Ministry Communities: Chaplains, Congregations, and Seminaries

JAMES M. SHOPSHIRE, SR.; MARK C. HICKS; AND RICHMOND STOGLIN

The connectional system of The United Methodist Church affords many avenues for advancing committed discipleship in restorative justice ministry. This is true even as we pursue new and more holistic approaches to prison ministry and criminal justice. In this book, we call attention to three ministry communities with primary roles in education, formation, and certification for restorative criminal justice ministry: chaplains, congregations, and seminaries. The General Board of Higher Education and Ministry and the General Board of Discipleship provide direct supervision of and support to these communities.

Prison chaplains, the first ministry community, are expected to have not only the foundational theological education required for ordained ministry but also more focused preparation required for official endorsement for the work of chaplaincy. Prison chaplains are endorsed through the United Methodist Endorsing Agency, a unit of the General Board of Higher Education and Ministry. The thirteen theological seminaries related to The United Methodist Church, the second ministry community, have heavy responsibility for providing high-quality theological education that helps prepare clergy and laity who serve in prison ministry and criminal justice work in various capacities.

The third ministry community comprises congregations and community-based groups. Both ordained clergy and laity are deployed from this community to ministry inside and outside prisons. This ministry community seeks to heal and restore those who have been wounded by criminal behavior (victims) and those who have served prison time (formerly incarcerated persons), seeking to facilitate healthy reentry into and responsible participation in the larger society.

In this chapter, we provide a brief introduction to each of these ministry communities, stressing the important role of each in a holistic approach to ministry with the incarcerated. We conclude with some practical suggestions that congregations, seminaries, chaplains, and the denomination as a whole can use to reinvigorate their commitment to vital prison ministry.

Endorsed Prison Chaplains and Restorative Justice

Richmond Stoglin

Life as a prison chaplain began for me in the spring of 1985. I was interviewed several times while waiting to be fully endorsed by The United Methodist Church. Most of my interviews took place within the federal prison, specifically the Federal Correctional Institution (FCI), Fort Worth, Texas, where I would be later assigned as an intern. Significantly, throughout the multiple interviews with the regional chaplain, stationed at FCI Fort Worth, I never felt afraid. Indeed, I felt so at home that I knew prison ministry was my calling. I chose to serve my career in field operations, which means being behind the bars with the inmates. During my nearly twenty-three year career, I served at FCI Seagoville, Texas (twice); FCI Texarkana, Texas; USP Lompoc, California; and as a member of the National Chaplains Response Team at FCI Oakdale, Louisiana, during the takeover riots by the Cuban detainees in November 1987. The fire of my original call still burns within me today.

There are no typical or routine days for a prison chaplain, even though there are set religious observances for each community. Imagine a building hosting religious services for Anglicans, Buddhists, Baptists, Catholics, Jews, Hindus, Methodists, Muslims, Native Americans, Nation of Islam, Rastafarians, Jehovah's Witnesses, Wiccas, and now Satanic worshipers—not to mention the off-shoots of these main religious communities! Each community having its own requirements and having to share space behind bars, when in the free world a lot of them did not even know of or acknowledge the other's existence. The chaplain is the one who has to manage this daily balancing act to avoid conflict within the prison. The inmates look to and respect the chaplain as a fair and impartial judge. It can become difficult for a chaplain to survive in such a setting if he or she does not have a strong sense of identity and a firmly grounded spiritual life. (One religious services department I was a part of coordinated religious services for twenty-eight religious communities and fifty-six services a week. We had approximately 130 active volunteers [none of whom, by the way, were United Methodists]).

Chaplains stationed inside institutions are called upon to fulfill not only "traditional" pastoral duties (Word and Sacrament) but also to serve as administrators; religious community coordinators; and logistics experts of materials, media, equipment, and people. Chaplains coordinate Bible studies and marriage institutes. In addition, they are required to know FAR (Federal Acquisition Regulations), JAR (Justice Acquisition Regulations), procurement procedures, draft statements of work for religious contractors (imams, rabbis, Native American medicine men), and more. A few years ago, the Federal Bureau of Prisons stopped the hiring of contract musicians for religious services. If a chaplain wants music, he or she has to procure either a volunteer from the civilian community or an inmate willing to play an instrument or to operate a DVD player. Additionally, chaplains are no longer allowed to solicit Bibles and other religious materials from organizations or institutions on the outside. To make things even more challenging, chaplains must often work without competent administrative assistance—or, at times, without an assistant at all. Chaplains have seen their work expand significantly since 9/11, with little additional support in sight. The combination of expanding duties and inadequate support is making recruitment of future chaplains increasingly challenging.

Many of these duties are difficult and yet deeply gratifying. At times chaplains help inmates who are believers negotiate the tension between their ultimate loyalty and their various limited loyalties. Here the wise chaplain does not seek to reduce or remove the tension but to help the inmate live with it in such a way that the conditional loyalties are kept open to the sanctions and resources of the Ultimate. While it would be too much to claim that the chaplain is the "conscience" of the institution, he or she does represent the quest for deeper moral and spiritual integrity by all persons in the institution.[1] The chaplain attempts to deliver all death notices, after proper verification. He or she allows inmates to call home and speak with family members upon receiving undesirable news. The chaplain facilitates the grieving process by allowing family members to send in video of funeral services to the chapel. The chapel provides them a safe environment to process their pain. The chaplain calls the inmates to the chapel, watches the videos with them, and assists them in understanding that it is normal to grieve the loss of a loved one.

The idea of a chaplain working to connect with inmates whose lives have been torn apart is something people who are not incarcerated can't fathom. For example, one eighteen year old, because of his life as a drug dealer, entered federal prison as a paraplegic due to a gunshot wound to his spine. After eighteen months he began attending services and activities in the Religious Services Department. In his desire to participate in the services, he learned how to read. He was released at age thirty-three and is actively pursuing opportunities to enter college and eventually attend seminary. His life became a living testimony of Christ's transforming power. He no longer sees his wheelchair as a handicap but as God's grace granting him an opportunity to change his life and affect the lives of others.

Being a chaplain is not easy. On many a day we feel like John the Baptist crying in the wilderness. On some days, when we feel pressure from those in the system who are unsympathetic to the possibility of spiritual transformation to be a law-enforcement officer rather than religious a confidant, the forward-thinking spirit of the apostle Paul lingers.

If The United Methodist Church wants to live out its commitment to prison ministry in the years ahead it must be deliberate about ordaining and endorsing clergy for this ministry. The need is urgent. Indeed, our denomination has come to a fork in the road with regard to our commitment to ministry in the criminal justice system in the United States. We can no longer afford to put our heads in the sand and expect the situation to improve on its own. Millions of people, families, and cultures in this nation are in need of a comprehensive plan to resolve the growing and menacing incarceration explosion. As I write these words, the volume of juveniles and women being incarcerated for violent crimes is escalating. Even a decade ago, we as a nation, a church, and as practicing Christians could not have imagined how increasing rates of violence among juveniles and women would lead to their increased incarceration. Without sounding alarmist, too many graves for young people have been dug. Also, too many cells have been built to warehouse people for crimes that are drug-related but not violent. To address this urgent situation requires deep commitment and deliberate action on the part of The United Methodist Church—and a critically important action is the recruitment, training, endorsement, and deployment of more chaplains in the correctional system.

Prison Ministry in Congregation and Community

Mark C. Hicks

The church of Jesus Christ is called to seek and save the lost and to heal and restore to wholeness all the people of God—*including* the victims and the perpetrators of crime. We tend to view the criminal justice system in abstract terms. Yet the church, like the criminal justice system, is made up of people. And many of the people in the criminal justice system come from our pews. Yes, *we* are the offenders and the offended. *We* are staff and inmates. *We* are both the victims and the perpetrators of crime. The church community is not isolated or immune from human sin—individually or collectively. The church stands in the midst of the sin, chaos, and confusion of the criminal justice system and cries out for justice. However, the church also stands with a precious gift to offer those within the criminal justice system—the gift of Christian ministry! The offering of that gift begins with visitation with incarcerated persons and victims of crime and extends to restoration and reentry into the community. Congregations and community-based organizations have a critical role to play in a holistic approach to prison ministry.

Today there are 2.3 million people in prison in the United States. This number exceeds the total population of many countries in the world. The United Methodist Church stands at the ready with a host of compassionate souls willing to do their part if given the proper tools and encouragement.

I am one of a growing number of United Methodists from the local church community who are engaged in prison ministry efforts. Together, we form a grassroots movement of lay and clergy volunteers with a desire to offer Christ to men, women, and youth behind stonewalls and razor wire.

Taken together, we are a large group. However, our service is as varied as the individuals that comprise this great cohort. We do our work through many programs and organizations: Disciple Bible Outreach Ministries of NC, Inc.; Prison Outreach Ministry of Western Pa.; Yokefellow Prison Ministries; Prison MATCH of NC, Inc.; Kairos Prison Ministry International; Epiphany Ministry, Inc.; Camp Hope; local church outreach; and many other efforts at restorative justice. Although our service is varied, our hearts are one. Our goal is ministry.

The good news is that United Methodists are increasingly becoming involved in prison ministry. This new wave of prison ministry is coming from the grassroots and is making itself known in many forms, from advocacy to hands-on efforts in the facilities. What accounts for this?

First, United Methodists are responding to the biblical mandate to visit those in prison. Christ reminds us: "I was in prison and you visited me"; and "just as you did it to one of the least of these who are members of my family, you did it to me." (Matt. 25:36, 40) In addition, the Great Commission calls us forth in ministry in the world: "Go therefore and make disciples of all nations, baptizing them in the name of the Father and of the Son and of the Holy Spirit, and teaching them to obey everything that I have commanded you. And remember, I am with you always, to the end of the age." (Matt. 28:19-20) Our faith is an active, seeking faith. We are no longer content to keep the faith in the sanctuary. We want to take it to a world in need.

Moreover, the ministry of Jesus as presented in Scripture reminds us of God's care and concern for the least, the last, and the lost. Consider the parables of the lost in Luke 15: the lost coin, the lost sheep, and the lost son. In these parables we find three different forms of lostness. The coin is lost through no fault of its own. The sheep is lost through its folly. The son is lost through his willful rebellion. Is this not also true of those we encounter in prison—people lost through injustice and abuse, whose upbringing and experiences contribute to their incarceration? Some are lost through no fault of their own. Others are lost through their folly. Still others are lost through their willful rebellion. Yet just as the father's love in the parable, God's love for them is stronger than their folly or rebellion. As the community called by the One who seeks and saves the lost, the church discovers ministry to the least of these at the core of its calling in the world.

Second, United Methodists are increasingly active in prison ministry because of the blessing we receive in return. I have long thought that prison ministry does more for the volunteer than for the inmate. In my work as Executive Director of Disciple Bible Outreach Ministries of NC, I have witnessed prison ministry transform the volunteers; and, as these people's lives are changed, so are their churches. Transformation takes place when we see the world more as Jesus sees it. As John Wesley has taught, by opening ourselves up in service to the Lord, our hearts are softened and we are drawn ever closer to the one who sent us. I have little doubt that the individuals who engage in prison ministry are the better for it. Likewise, I know that their churches are stronger, for they have a greater awareness of the world around them and an increased compassion for those for whom Jesus died.

Third, as United Methodist people, we are finally coming to terms with our Wesleyan heritage of prison ministry. In Chapter 5, Richard Heitzenrater paints a compelling picture of the central place of prison ministry in John Wesley's outreach to the larger community. Every time a United Methodist enters a prison for ministry, he or she becomes a part of this significant legacy. More recently, a United Methodist bishop has said that a United Methodist minister should be as familiar with the inside of a prison cell as with the inside of a hospital room.

But prison ministry has never been reserved for the clergy alone. As United Methodists, we need to rediscover Sarah Peters, a devoted early Methodist who regularly visited the prisons. In fact, so committed was Peters that she gave her life for the cause, contracting from her visits what was known at the time as "jail fever"—a disease that eventually claimed her life.[2] From the earliest days of the Methodist societies, lay and clergy alike have joined in prison ministry efforts. This venerable history continues into our time.

Commenting on the staggering size of the current U.S. prison population, Bishop Richard Wilke observes: "If we had a country of 2,000,000 persons, we would send missionaries to that country. Why don't we say the same about prisons? This too is a mission field."

Why should congregations engage in prison ministry? Our Scripture, our need for personal transformation, and our Wesleyan heritage require it. Someone has said that the next great revival in the United States will come out of the prisons. Who knows whether this will happen? But one thing is certain: Prison ministry changes lives. May the groundswell in prison ministry continue; and may a great revival come, not only to our prisons but also to our churches!

United Methodist Seminaries and Theological Education

James M. Shopshire, Sr.

To faithfully participate in a vision of restorative justice takes creative, bold leadership. For United Methodists, education in general, and theological education in particular, has long been the primary means of preparing people for creative and committed service. Thus, the seminaries, the church's specialized academies for equipping clergy (and increasingly laity), play a critical role in preparing men and women for a full range of ministries.

Yet, why are there so few United Methodists educated to serve in restorative justice ministry with a focus on the criminal justice system? Why are so many pastors unaware of injustice associated with the prison-industrial complex and unprepared to serve the needs of individuals, families, and communities when people are affected by the criminal justice system? Even more troublesome is the tendency among many United Methodists not to want to bother with people who, for reasons real or contrived, are processed through the criminal justice system. Why is there reluctance to touch offenders and to speak and work proactively on behalf of incarcerated people who have too little access to rights, representation, and resources to defend themselves? How can we do the personal and pastoral work of prison ministry without losing sight of the prophetic call for changes in social policy toward social justice?

One reason for the distancing of leaders and members from criminal justice concerns and prison ministry is insufficient exposure to the sociocultural realities of local, national, and global contexts. While our Wesleyan heritage has always emphasized the importance of personal and social holiness, we have tended to hold fast to the personal and to relinquish the call for acts of mercy and justice in the society. United Methodists, too, experience the increased fear and suspicion concerning crime and corrections that affect our daily lives in the twenty-first century. This fact does not bode well for a denomination's witness whose history and heritage are strong on social holiness.

It is at this critical juncture that seminaries have a pivotal role to play. The thirteen United Methodist theological seminaries and schools of theology are a critical link in equipping ministers who can raise awareness and prepare others to engage in the ministry of justice that transforms and restores people and communities to wholeness and wholesomeness. Of all the contributing educational institutions, the seminaries are essential for the translation, analysis, interpretation, and application of the faith of the church to the experiences of everyday life. Every person who graduates from seminary should be able to do a basic social analysis of real-life situations. Otherwise, he or she is not ready for leadership among the people of God, the church. As a matter of fact, if one cannot or does not do critical social analysis before making theological pronouncements, one cannot be faithful and effective in ministry that is set within a network of social relationships in the midst of community and society.

The seminaries are the specialized institutions for educating— *not* training—persons for ministry. However, seminaries tend to major in preparing persons for generalized ministry, primarily in congregational settings. Focused, community-based ministry and ministry in institutional settings are left dependent less on educational curricula and more on the talent and commitment of those who feel called to pursue ministries such as chaplaincy (prison, hospital, military, campus, etc.). It is not difficult to discern that annual conferences and their episcopal leaders tend to place more emphasis on educating clergy for service in the local church than for ministries outside denominational structures. This is the case, in part, because many worthy structures of ministry contribute little or nothing to the baseline support of The United Methodist Church.

The United Methodist Church today struggles with the reality that appointments to extension ministry remove persons from the administrative and financial routines of the annual conference and local churches. And because they are the major avenues for the degrees and certifications required for appointment to local churches, seminaries tend to focus their resources on preparing pastors of local churches. Preparation for prison chaplaincy most likely comes from selective studies in the core curricula of the seminaries.

It is worth asking how the seminaries have fared in educating persons for chaplaincy, in general, and for prison chaplaincy, in particular.

Generally speaking, seminaries tend to prepare seminarians either for service in the local church or for teaching and research. Persons in a Master of Divinity degree program who believe themselves to be called to serve in settings other than congregation or classroom are largely required to piece together educational programs and hope for approval as they advance through the candidacy process.

As previously stated, the seminaries and schools of theology represent one of the ministry communities with a stake in and considerable responsibility for criminal justice ministry in prisons and in church and community settings. Although rarely on the front lines of prison ministry, the seminaries are called to play an important role in preparing ministers who take the lead in this vital ministry.

To take this leadership role, seminaries must pay careful attention to their partners and constituencies in the work of prison ministry as they consider staffing, curriculum development, and other opportunities for educational formation. First, seminaries must be responsive to the needs and requirements of various agencies of the church. The General Board of Higher Education and Ministry and its endorsing agency for chaplaincies illustrates the point. Conversation between the seminaries and GBHEM is ongoing with regard to extension ministries such as prison ministry and criminal justice. While largely cooperative and consultative, such conversations connect seminaries with the larger scope of the denomination's mission and ministry, providing important information for adjusting curricula and assigning institutional and financial resources.

Annual conference boards of ordained ministry represent another critical partner in the connectional system with whom communication and conversation is important. Moreover, other boards and agencies within the United Methodist connectional structure interact with seminaries regarding specialized extension ministries. They, too, must navigate the currents of what can and cannot reasonably fit into core curricula of the seminaries. Then there are relationships to accrediting agencies outside the church structures, such as the Association of Theological Schools (ATS), each with its own interests and demands.

As noted earlier, there is a dearth of endorsed prison chaplains in The United Methodist Church. As the third-largest Christian denomination in the United States and the second-largest Protestant denomination, The United Methodist Church reported only thirty-six endorsed chaplains in 2007. Of these, a mere six serve within the Federal Bureau of Prisons. The remaining thirty chaplains serve in various state prisons and county jails. Besides these endorsed persons are a number of non-endorsed United Methodist chaplains who volunteer to serve in local jails and community ministries along with an indeterminate number of local clergy and lay volunteers who serve as "outside/inside" volunteers for ministry. It is difficult to estimate their exact number. However, this pattern of modest recruitment and preparation for the endorsed prison chaplaincy and indeterminate certification of other volunteers inevitably raises the question of the denomination's and its seminaries' level of commitment to prison and criminal justice ministry.

My recent cursory look at catalog offerings of the thirteen United Methodist seminaries over the past several years shows few courses specifically devoted to restorative justice with specific reference to criminal justice and prison ministry. A full-blown study would be necessary to accurately determine the extent to which prison ministry and criminal justice offerings were made and in what relationship to a restorative justice paradigm. Yet my quick review yielded interesting insights. Three seminaries had scheduled offerings on religion, society, and justice issues. One seminary offered a course on the ethical task and justice ministry. The preponderance of seminary courses related to general preparation for ministry within congregations. A course here and there might incorporate references to prison and criminal justice ministry. Virtually all of the seminaries offered courses that dealt generally with pastoral care and counseling. It is not immediately apparent whether some of the courses gave focus to counseling incarcerated people and their families or pastoral caring for reentry ministry. Even more difficult to determine was the extent to which there was understanding of the economic and policy nexus in assessing punishment in the criminal justice system. I had difficulty in identifying courses that dealt explicitly with the biblical and theological foundations for justice ministry or in finding non-degree courses and programs that offer certification in prison ministry for laity and clergy. Although significant programs may exist, it is rare to find seminary programs that are designed to deal with ministry to, with, and to some degree, against, the criminal justice system. Much work remains to be done in this area.

Three Communities—One Ministry

And so, the three ministry communities intersect in a shared vision of wide-reaching, growing, holistic prison and criminal justice ministry in The United Methodist Church. The observation that there has not been enough comprehensive work with a qualitative social justice emphasis is not intended to diminish the sincere and growing efforts in criminal justice ministry.

This book holds out the prospect of vital presence of United Methodists inside prisons among the incarcerated and outside among ex-offenders reentering society. The outside context is the focal point where restoration is lived out in its fullness, where persons and families of the wounded and families of the formerly incarcerated seek reunion and renewal for sharing in the larger community.

Ideally, each ministry community has critical responsibility in every aspect of criminal justice ministry. Endorsed chaplains, inside and outside; local congregation and community ministers, outside and inside; and seminaries—working together to raise consciousness and to equip all ministers for effective service.

Much remains to be done to strengthen the three ministry communities in the work of restorative justice, particularly with reference to criminal justice and prison ministry. The endorsed chaplaincy has served competently but with declining personnel and impetus for prison ministry. Congregations have been involved more heavily in Bible study and pastoral aspects of prison ministry but with an anemic interpretive principle as a guide. Advocacy and action to reform structural and systemic aspects of the prison and criminal justice system have been less apparent and in most cases absent. United Methodist seminaries have continued to equip generalists for ministry with congregations. Educating persons for specialized institutional ministries such as prison chaplaincy has received little emphasis thus far. Nor has enough intellectual effort gone into social teaching that sheds light on the issues and informs and equips the church to address the way criminal justice is pursued in community and society.

Given the critical, crisis-level proportions of crime and the misappropriations of the cultures and criminal justice systems of the United States, The United Methodist Church is challenged to intentional renewal of its ministry for restorative justice. How might congregations, chaplains, and seminaries help the church respond to this challenge? We mention just a few possibilities. Local churches might begin by considering the following suggestions: (1) Become aware of the correctional institutions in their areas. (2) Visit those institutions and learn about the people incarcerated there, those who work as administrators and staff, those who legislate the way federal, state, and local institutions should operate, those who are renewed and return to the community, and those who otherwise profit from or lose out on prison institutions. (3) Help recruit committed, well-educated ministers who will faithfully serve the church as chaplains and ministers inside prisons and outside in the communities to which most incarcerated persons return. (4) Reclaim our Wesleyan heritage in prison ministry and look for ways to live it out concretely in our time. (5) Draw upon the Scriptures as primary resource for faithful and effective discipleship. (6) Volunteer and help recruit others to work as agents of edification and transformation in prisons and outside in congregations and communities.

Chaplains, too, can play an important role. (1) They can increase their own awareness of local congregations near the location of prisons and jails with the prospect of developing mutual ministry. (2) Within the limits of their assignments in prison institutions, chaplains can serve as resources to churches on the outside through workshops, preaching and speaking engagements, and leading discussion groups on the criminal justice system. (3) Chaplains can serve as key resources in helping United Methodist pastors and congregations understand important problems, needs, and issues in prison systems and encouraging local churches and annual conferences to shape strategic plans for recruitment and support of endorsed chaplains in The United Methodist Church.

United Methodist seminaries have distinctive contributions to make: (1) As the church's academies, seminaries can give leadership in forging curricular offerings and programs for formation of various restorative ministers and ministries. (2) They can help to better equip the church and its ministry to deal with justice issues, with a socio-logic and a theo-logic that makes contact with concrete situations in life. (3) With support from the whole connectional system, the seminaries can fulfill the critical role of consciousness-raising and developing increasing socio-theological competency for restorative justice ministry. Such competency has broad implications specifically for criminal justice and prison ministry as well as generally in light of the whole ministry of the church.

One matter is increasingly apparent. In order for holistic ministry to grow stronger the ministry communities must work cooperatively and support one another. Together they represent a cadre of leadership for the whole United Methodist Church. Through the three ministry communities comes a promise for more effective service in the many facets of criminal justice ministry.

NOTES

1. M. Greenburg, "Prison." *The Interpreter's Dictionary of the Bible*, ed. George A. Buttrick (Nashville: Abingdon, 1962), 891–92.

2. John Wesley, *The Works of John Wesley*. The Bicentennial Edition. Ed. Richard P. Heitzenrater and W. Reginald Ward (Nashville: Abingdon, 1991), 20:340.

Section 2

Biblical and Socio-Theological Perspectives

CHAPTER 3

A Socio-logic for a Theology of Prison Ministry

JAMES M. SHOPSHIRE, SR.

A widespread assumption in the church is that we can read our Bibles, say our prayers, and proceed directly to effective ministry. United Methodists need to be disabused of that idea. *The ministry of the church is always worked out in social context.* As a result, it is necessary to observe and learn as much as possible about the social context of life before plunging in to engage or otherwise change it. To those who say, "There you go again with that social gospel stuff," I say, "The gospel *is* social." The gospel is about good news and wholesome, just relationships between God and God's people.

Ministry cannot be relevant in isolation from the social context of people and their needs. Ministry cannot be aloof, only occasionally touching people where they live. Trying to make the appearance of being down to earth, without walking with people on the ground, does not work. It is in the midst of the people that Jesus came and served, healed and set free those imprisoned by others in the very real circumstances of their lives. It is to the same places that the church must follow for faithful and effective ministry.

John Wesley fully realized the social nature of the gospel in his ministry. He insisted on striving for personal holiness, covenantal disciplines, and vital piety but also clearly understood that caring for the souls of people was only part of the ministry. One had to care for those who were sent to the debtor's prison, those who labored all their lives in mines and fields, those whose only relief from their situation in life was to waste away vital resources in the pub.

United Methodists who are suspicious of the relevance to the Christian church of a social gospel message and ministry are invited to experience immersion in the biblical text again. The invitation calls for a journey through the Old and New Covenants and through the heritage transmitted from John and Charles Wesley in order to reassess the meaning for United Methodists at the present time. As with Jesus of Nazareth, Wesley's analysis of the life in community informed his preaching and his ministry to people in the society.

Essential streams of logic run through the message and ministry of the church. For many, the notion of "logic" seems to have little to do with what they believe and, therefore, is not important to guide their lives as Christians. However, rejecting the need for logical thought threatens to remove focused and critical thinking from the realm of believing and leaves faithful Christians stranded with unreflective beliefs.

By definition, logic is concerned with "reason or sound judgment, as in utterances or actions," or "a particular method of reasoning or argumentation."[1] When we talk about God—who God is, what God has done, what God is doing—we use a "theo-logic" that reflects on God's action in the lives and relationships of humankind. When we talk about society and social life—social needs, social actions and interactions, social problems, social issues, social change, and how we live together responsibly or irresponsibly—we use a "socio-logic." In matters of faith and action, a socio-logic is separable from a theo-logic. They converge and merge, and constantly interact with each other, as the biblical narratives already attest (see Figure 1, p. 31).

John Wesley understood this dynamic well. While he was not a social analyst in contemporary terms and, apparently, did not entertain comprehensive notions of fundamental societal change in

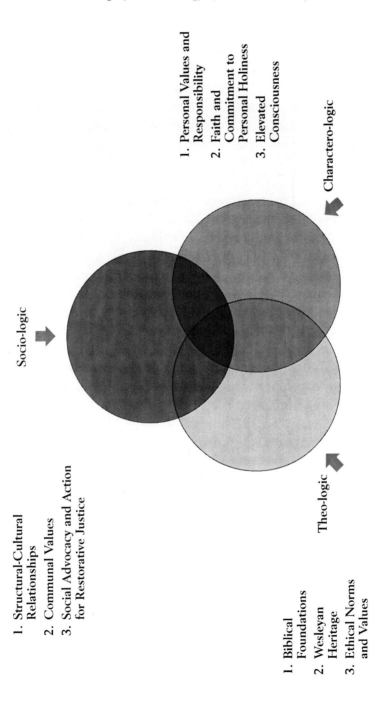

Figure 1: Converging Logics of Ministry with the Criminal Justice System

Socio-logic

1. Structural-Cultural Relationships
2. Communal Values
3. Social Advocacy and Action for Restorative Justice

Charactero-logic

1. Personal Values and Responsibility
2. Faith and Commitment to Personal Holiness
3. Elevated Consciousness

Theo-logic

1. Biblical Foundations
2. Wesleyan Heritage
3. Ethical Norms and Values

England, his preaching and his ministry within and beyond the church employed a socio-logic that understood the plight of the poor and lower classes and sought to respond to their needs. Wesley and the Methodists saw the need for reform with regard to poverty, law, and the penal system. (See Chapter 5 for an in-depth treatment of Wesley's prison ministry.) Of course, reform did not equate to fundamental social change. Indeed, some historians maintain that Wesley and the Methodist movement contributed to a lessening of revolutionary fervor for societal change in England at a time when other European countries were experiencing major upheavals.

However, for Wesley, the quest for social reform did not end with concern for the penal system alone. The theme of social holiness extended to the institution of slavery. Despite a flawed anthropology relative to African peoples and peoples on other continents perceived to be different and, therefore, inferior to Europeans, John and Charles Wesley were prophetic concerning the degrading consequences of slavery and spoke out against it. They did this not as sociologists but as men of faith.[2] The Wesleys' efforts at reform reveal an ample socio-logic based on the truth of the gospel.

The essential point here is the meaning and function of "logic" as a way of thinking about life, faith, and action. An adequate socio-logic is necessary for the theological and ethical task of responding to God in faithful and effective ministry. Ministry without understanding of the social context is limited in its ability to truly connect with God's transformative and restorative mission.

Socio-Theological Assumptions for Prison Ministry and Criminal Justice

My argument in this chapter proceeds on the basis of several assumptions about the socio-theological and ethical task for doing ministry with, for, and sometimes in opposition to the people and patterned relationships that constitute the criminal justice system. First, while some biblical passages respond directly to the difficult questions about justice (Micah, Hosea) in the midst of community, the whole Bible is an authoritative resource for understanding what is just and righteous before God and within the human community.

Biblical references to prisons show imprisonment as punishment for a variety of offenses, including political purposes of repression and control, the inability of the poor to support themselves, individuals' inability to meet the demands of taxation imposed by wealthy controlling or occupying powers, and resisting exploitation. The biblical witness makes clear that such imprisonment runs counter to the good news of the gospel and the divine intention of care, redemption, and release of human beings.

Scripture records a range of forms of punishment for various offenses against the community (including murder [Lev. 24:12-23]), from detention to the death penalty. The overarching tone is for just treatment, healthy measures of correction, and healing in the human situation (Ezra 7:21-26; Matt. 25:36; Luke 3:18-20; 4:18; Acts 12:1-5; 16:25-31; 22:19; Heb. 13:3). The creative, redemptive, and sustaining work of God provides the original example of just treatment, healthy correction, and healing. John Wesley and his brother Charles emulated God's mission and in the process provided a human example of faithfulness passed on to us in the witness of those people called Methodists.

The message inherent in the biblical references above affirms the intrinsic worth of all humanity as God's people in the world. Despite all, people are worth saving. The final word among the faithful should be that justice in the land rests upon discernment of appropriate sanctions devised by humankind as a participation in and emulation of God's saving work of love, peace, justice, mercy, and grace in the full range of human relationships.

The biblical notion of jubilee justice adds a further dimension to this perspective. Liberation from servitude is like release from prison, like captives being set free. The Scriptures variously show that servitude has long been a form of imprisonment through which labor is unjustly extracted from people who have no other means of earning a livelihood.

The second assumption is that justice always has communal aspects. That is, justice has to do with building relationships that contribute to the edification of persons as members of the human family and to strengthening the beloved community. Justice cannot be effectively dispensed for individuals who have no recourse other than to live in communities with relational structures that institutionalize and perpetuate injustice. Hence, when dealing with the issues of incarceration and criminal justice, both positive and negative sanctions are tools for fulfilling personal and communal values that are consistently directed away from the punitive destruction of body, mind, and spirit and toward the fulfillment of freedom, justice, and equality.

Third, the oppressive weight of the material and spiritual wealth gap both conditions and distorts outcomes regarding justice. If persons or groups do not have access to money and power they most likely will not receive "what is due" them. Such a state of affairs flies in the face of the radical principle of equality before God that undergirds the faith premises of most of the world's religions and of Christian faith in particular.

The fourth and final assumption is that the *socio-logical, charactero-logical,* and *theo-logical* aspects of our quest for relevant ministry pertaining to criminal justice all converge to demand profound responses from those who would be the people of God. Prophetic and priestly advocacy and action toward the ends of justice for all—including criminals—in the contexts of national and global communities are altogether consistent with creative and responsible ministry.

The socio-logical, charactero-logical, and theo-logical aspects form an integrated matrix that needs always to be held together for effective ministry to take place. Taken by themselves, social analysis and interpretation of the conditions in prisons, in the justice and correctional systems, and in church and society, mean little. The constant struggle is to be in ministry with meaning, engaging people and structures in such manner that movement toward the ends of justice will always be part of our faith journey. Similarly, focusing merely on the character of incarcerated persons, prison administrators, judges, police personnel, endorsed prison chaplains on the inside, prison ministers going in from the outside, or seminary teachers or administrators without a growing awareness of the personal and interpersonal matrix that binds them together will not lead to valuable ministry. Theological interpretation—the third part of the matrix—

is critically important to guide us to reflection, proclamation, advocacy and action. It comes alive only in relationship to our level of consciousness and the quality of our discernment, nourishing courage and energy to engage the issues of criminal justice.

In order to effectively engage the challenge of developing ministry that is sociologically relevant and theologically grounded in an understanding of restorative justice, United Methodists would do well to attend to these four assumptions. Such ministry must reach out to *all* the actors within the relational matrix. Only in so doing will the church participate meaningfully in the transformation of incarcerated offenders, the healing of people whom they have hurt, as well as the restoration of the larger pattern of relationships in community and society.

Access to accurate and timely information is basic. Detailed information is essential and readily available for the work of restorative ministry that is both personal and social. Such information enables United Methodists to ask the appropriate questions in formation for ministry. For example, why has incarceration of people in prisons and jails sharply increased in the United States over the past thirty years? A 500 percent increase has resulted in a total of 2.3 million people in prison.[3] The United States imprisons more people than any other nation, including China, which incarcerates an estimated 1.5 million people.[4] The United States proudly claims a 232-year national heritage of governance that values life, liberty, and democratic freedoms with a population that recently passed 300 million. Yet China, with a population exceeding 1.3 billion people, and with a mixed heritage of governance over the past two centuries through more restrictive patterns of economy and polity, incarcerates fewer people than the United States.[5]

Other questions persist. Why does approximately 50 percent of the prison population consist of Black people, who make up only 13 percent of the U.S. population? Increasing numbers of Latinos/ Hispanics are processed through the criminal justice system. Color and immigrant status no doubt play a significant role. Juveniles, women, and the poor are increasingly subjected to punishment in the system that purports to punish or correct people toward the ends of justice. What is the correlation between poverty and imprisonment? Why are there more Blacks than Whites on death row? Why are there only a handful of Black prosecutors? Why are there so few endorsed United Methodist chaplains—particularly Black chaplains—working with the Federal Bureau of Prisons? These questions barely scratch the surface of the issues about criminal justice and prisons confronting the nation and the church.

An indispensable resource for United Methodists is the *Book of Resolutions*, updated at General Conference every four years. No preparation for ministry with prisoners and prisons and for criminal justice will be adequate without consulting this book of guidelines. Particularly important are the Social Principles, which represent the denomination's framework for deliberation on a whole range of ethical and moral issues. Studying these principles, along with the relevant resolutions on criminal justice, is an excellent way to gain a fuller understanding of what is required for participation in God's redemptive mission in the world.

Until we who would be the church are willing to do the social analysis that informs and empowers the work with the criminal justice system, we cannot truly be the faithful people of God. The chapters in this book illustrate various concrete ways of responding to the responsibility of being instruments of grace for restorative justice.

A Socio-logic that Informs a Theo-logic in Prison Ministry

Perhaps the most challenging question facing the church in its ministry with the criminal justice system is this: How can the church's restorative ministry be extended with integrity when the prevailing meaning system and ultimate decision-making authority reside in another institutional setting? Put differently, how can the church truly be the church when the preponderant goal and mission of the prison or jail—or even the criminal justice system as a whole—are inconsistent with the restorative work of the Christian gospel? Consider, for example, the role of the prison chaplain. The commanding officer or chief administrator of the prison is the final arbiter of what a denomination and its chaplains are permitted to do.

Consequently, chaplains often find themselves restricted to doing "pastoral" work and excluded from affecting decisions about the institution's purpose, order, operations, and discipline. This issue affects not only prison ministry but also other extension ministries, such as the military.

Ministry in such settings will always be subject to limitations imposed by officials in the host institutions. The task of the church is to discern the shape and role that its pastoral and prophetic ministry should take within these boundaries. Often the church's ability to prophetically challenge host organizations is restricted, but that does not keep it from exercising its pastoral role. Often the pastoral role, well performed, enhances the prophetic influence. Over the years, I have come to a greater understanding and appreciation of prison chaplaincy as a ministry of presence, proclamation, and pastoral caring for people at both individual and group levels. Ministry with those on the inside has the potential of personal, pastoral, and restorative influence, even if subdued by the overall purpose of the institution.

Much in the biblical narratives suggests that the church's priestly and pastoral function should always be present wherever any of God's people are located. This is believed to be true, whether in the courts of kings and rulers or on battlefields, in sacred places or on journeys through valleys of the shadow of death. The church's story proclaims that any person or system that reaches to touch the hem of Jesus' garment can be renewed as a result of the encounter with divine love and justice. A thorough socio-logic of transformation and restoration understands that healing and renewing power opens possibilities for persons and for larger systems of life.

And so, it is necessary to develop a socio-logic that informs our theo-logic so that we have the guidance and insight to deal with real issues—from pastoral challenges to policy matters—that arise both inside and outside the prison walls. Interaction between an adequate socio-logic and a grounded theo-logic is of great importance in the ministry with incarcerated people and their families, with victims and their families, and with those who do ministry within various aspects of the criminal justice system, community and society at-large. In the midst of it all, we know that God promises to be present with us, using us as agents of nurture, enlightenment, healing, and restoration.

Important Factors in an Active Socio-logic for Ministry

An operational socio-logic for criminal justice and prison ministry leads one to deal with different factors that add or detract from the restorative process. At least two factors require attention. First, an adequate operating socio-logic takes seriously the need to minister to the *person* and to the *circumstances* that contribute to his or her situation in life. Bible study or vibrant worship experiences alone are not sufficient to open up a range of redemptive possibilities. Given what can be learned about the offender's life, the minister on the outside of prison walls or counselor or brother can assist with organizing experiences and resources to help a person reenter community without falling into circumstances and behaviors that lead to recidivism.

In the ministry of the church, restorative justice initiatives should be extended to ex-offenders and to victims. Preoccupation with punishment of offenders often results in oversight and neglect of victims. By the same token, failure to address the needs and problems of persons victimized by crime leaves bitter residues that inhibit health recovery. Restorative justice reaches out to all involved and, in so doing, provides healing to each and to the whole community. This is a profound element of the church's ministry.

Second, an operating socio-logic sets the goal of progressive movement from presence to pastoral caring to prophetic announcement. The more expansive part of a socio-logic of ministry is the development of proactive response to demonstrated need, a voice of advocacy in word and deed, and *policy* action to change the law to aid in the restoration of individuals and society. Each aspect is important, and none can be omitted. The five aspects of ministry are set forth in Figure 2 below.

Ministries of *presence* necessarily radiate out to all characters and structures in the prison and criminal justice ministry. Presence is

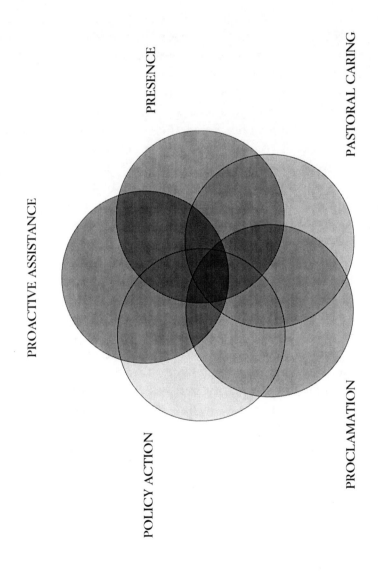

Figure 2: Five Critical Aspects of Criminal Justice Ministry

PRESENCE

PASTORAL CARING

PROACTIVE ASSISTANCE

POLICY ACTION

PROCLAMATION

another way of speaking about being where incarcerated people are located and victims are recovering. Being present is more than the visit to prison for worship and Bible study. It is more than making connection with families and assisting with bridging relationships between offenders and families. Presence includes being there when important decisions are being made. It means being there for the long term, when prisoners are released and need help in getting reestablished in employment and housing.

Presence also means being there for the victims of crime. Pain, discouragement, and loss associated with criminal victimization are usually dealt with alone. Being there as the church through the lonely process of recovery from loss is not primarily a singing and praying event. Discernment of need and making connection with people who suffer from brokenness of body, mind, and spirit can sometimes be better accomplished with being seen, a gentle touch to communicate a caring countenance, and a closed mouth to allow important sounds of silence to be heard.

Presence is being there when a word of support and encouragement needs to be spoken with criminal justice authorities that are looking and listening for signs and indications that transformation is taking place and release to new freedom is appropriate for incarcerated persons. Ministry of presence has many aspects that can creatively and responsibly contribute to the restoration of lives and the renewal of systems intended to foster recovery.

Pastoral caring is connected to and yet separate from a ministry of presence. Foresight and insight become important tools for ministering to incarcerated persons—people who need help in healing their own broken existence.

Proclamation, along with study and edification, are high points of the church's ministry in prisons. Proclamation and study must be placed in perspective and not viewed as the totality of prison ministry. In The United Methodist Church, as in most Christian communions, more people are engaged with prisoners through visitation, study, and preaching than any other single form of ministry. And while these efforts are commendable, they are not enough. I call this level of engagement the "personalistic-pastoral" beginning of prison ministry; it needs to evolve into several other levels of involvement. For its completion, the priestly-pastoral mode of proclamation is followed by the prophetic-transformational mode.

Proactive ministry of service takes on great importance at the time former prisoners reenter the community. Clothes and a few dollars after exiting prison gates are too little to sustain a person who is coming out. Housing, medical and health considerations, employment, support, and mentoring are critical needs that, if left unmet, lead to recidivism.

Policy action is a level of criminal justice ministry that few undertake. The demands are great and many of the would-be-faithful do not understand, consider the risks too great, or do not feel that efforts to reform prison policy are the true work of the church. John Wesley would be saddened by such a view. Advocacy of prison reform was as much a part of prison ministry as regular prison visitations, as Richard Heitzenrater's chapter indicates.

Without a doubt, the need for policy reform and paradigm shifts in broad aspects of the criminal justice system is great. Differences and disparities in treatment persist and increase in numerous areas; for example, in terms of arrests; sentencing guidelines; capital punishment; treatment of juveniles, women, the poor (as in Wesley's time); seniors; matters of sexuality and sexual orientation; rise of market-based private prisons; the location of prisons; problems related to prison guards, their families, and the communities in which they are located. All of these are subject to policy review for restorative justice.

Putting a Socio-logic of Criminal Justice and Prison Ministry to Work

A church that seeks to construct a working socio-logic of criminal justice ministry would do well to attend to five components of effective prison ministry. I list and briefly discuss each below.

1. Taking Stock Through Critical Social Analysis

A thoroughgoing socio-logic always begins with an examination of what is actually the situation or issue at hand. Appearances can be misleading. Stakeholders and powerbrokers can misunderstand or misrepresent the real issues. Victims are often neglected or compelled to pursue punitive action when they or the community would be better served through restitution and reconciliation of relationships. Critical social analysis is an important tool for asking the appropriate questions in the quest for personal and social justice and well-being.

Inherent in every criminal justice issue is the need to understand the economic, political, cultural, and relational implications for all of the people involved. This includes the victim and the offender, as well as everyone involved or impacted by the process—from the offender to the prosecutor; from the victim to the judge; from the chaplains on the inside to the supportive ministers, volunteers, and congregations on the outside. Critical analysis asks what are the legal—and, just as important, the theo-logical and ethical—values and principles the church should bring to its work in prison and criminal justice? Figure 3 below illustrates the range and scope of interactions to be considered.

2. Assessing the Relative Impact on People: Who Pays and Who Benefits?

Criminal justice ministry and restorative justice initiatives must give attention to victims and those variously offended. Restorative justice quite appropriately directs attention to the care and healing of the victims. Next, it moves to the question of restitution in an effort to restore the life and relational well-being of offenders. Last, it considers how the community can benefit from restoration to wholeness as contrasted with severe, extended, and permanent measures of punishment.

Unfortunately, the focus of federal, state, and local criminal justice systems is almost entirely on the individual offender and how best to exact punishment on behalf of the state. Disparities in sentencing based on race and ethnicity tell a troublesome story about who pays and who benefits. Another unfortunate aspect of the prevailing focus is the systemic tendency to go all out to put the corner drug dealer or small-time bank robber away for a long time while

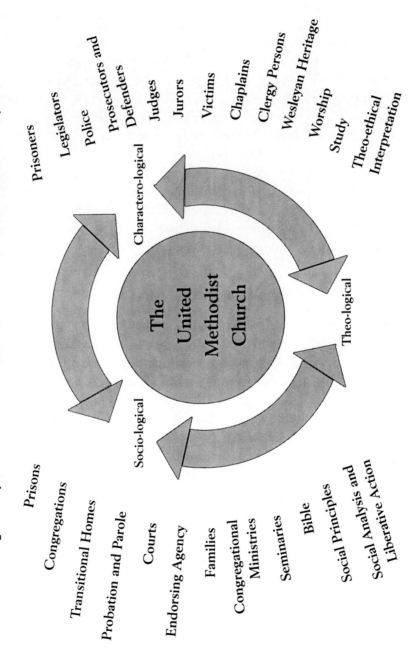

Figure 3: Dynamic Personal and Structural Relations in Criminal Justice Ministry

being more restrained and unduly favorable toward large-scale importers of illegal drugs or the perpetrators of billion-dollar frauds, which damage thousands of people in a single operation.

The question of who pays and how much is paralleled by the question of who benefits and by how much. In recent years, offenders incarcerated through the criminal justice system have often become a cheap source of labor, adding considerable income to state and local jurisdictions.[6] Prison towns, exploitation of internal prison labor, private prisons, and a growing list of benefits to the prison industry have been documented in recent years.[7] The same benefits are said to accrue for communities that host large prisons, providing jobs for people often displaced from other parts of the job market. Only careful examination will reveal whether the benefits to communities actually outweigh the human costs.

3. Discerning and Developing Strategies for Restorative Justice

It is clear by now that United Methodists have ample resources from our heritage to lead and participate in measures of restorative justice. Engaging in prison ministry in a meaningful way takes both discernment and strategic action—and United Methodists should draw on their biblical and theological heritage in this process. As noted earlier, restorative justice is more than a concept; it is a framework for approaching prison ministry. Understanding this framework will require careful, sustained discernment. This framework serves as the context for developing concrete strategies of constructive interaction with criminal justice institutions. As the late Harmon Wray points out in his book *Restorative Justice: Moving Beyond Punishment,* while restorative justice is not a specific program or course of action, it does identify the principles upon which effective intervention can be built.

> Restorative justice is a wide-ranging movement that seeks to transform existing systems for dealing with interpersonal and intergroup conflict. Rooted in older, indigenous, tribal traditions of community justice, and in the biblical traditions of *shalom,*

44

Jubilee economics, and the Sermon on the Mount, restorative justice refocuses our gaze and reshapes the questions and assumptions that underlie our retributive system. It seeks to deinstitutionalize abstract and ineffective systems of jurisprudence and replace them with practical action by concrete, grassroots communities. . . . Restorative justice is not a program, or a specific way of doing things, although there are, of course, programs consistent with its principles. It is, rather, a perspective, a point of view, a focus from which we can better understand the realities of crime and punishment in our society. Restorative justice represents what philosophers call a "paradigm shift," or a change in explanatory models, in how to think about crime, violence, and conflict—and how to respond.[8]

Too many congregations approach ministry from the vantage point of people who are comfortable and insulated socio-economically from common people as well as "common criminals." Many of these parishioners are distrustful and fearful of so-called "crime in the streets" and avoid contact with citizens who seem more likely to be involved in criminal behaviors. Thus, people who live in poverty and struggle for subsistence are criminalized, with little distinction made between their survival behaviors and their plight due to criminal victimization.

Suspicion and avoidance of people who are racially or culturally different and economically less well off receive social reinforcement by separation mechanisms built into the social fabric of communities. Many socially well-to-do people consider swift and severe punishment the only way to deal with criminal offenders. For them, seeking restoration and restitution smacks of "coddling" criminals. For some, the very idea of ministry with offenders and ex-offenders is conditioned by an attitude not of restoration but of protecting oneself from perceived and real threats. It is not uncommon for such folk to distinguish between "common criminals" of the street variety, who are more likely to commit crimes of personal victimization, and "white collar" criminals, who are more likely to commit crimes of mass victimization against the community and society.

When elites and middle-class people decide to get involved, they tend to choose in advance what the situational needs and issues are for those who break the law. Their assistance most likely takes the form of admonitions, prayers, and the occasional charitable handout. Often they hold up their own lifestyles of wealth, influence, and power as models for the poor, incarcerated people to imitate. Unfortunately, this is not unusual. In virtually all cases where ministry involves a group so different that their helpers simply do not understand their situation (poor, working poor, racial-ethnics, women, children, sexual orientation, etc.), the tendency is for the helpers to decide what the recipients of their generosity need, or to do something quickly and leave, or to blame the recipients for failing to improve.

The same pattern shows up in relation to restorative justice and criminal justice ministry. Once those with rigid attitudes of "do the time if you do the crime" enter the conversation, the recriminations against all offenders escalate. The "get tough on criminals" attitude, with its increasingly obvious bias, looms larger as the best and only way to deal with crime and punishment. Such sentiments enter into the voting booth and become the currency for election of policy-making authority. Narrow attitudes and prescriptions for restorative justice are no more helpful in the community of faith and the community-at-large than a dismissive attitude that relieves people of all responsibility for their conduct in the life of the community.

Many physical crimes against persons occur within a particular racial-ethnic group (Black,[9] White, Hispanic, Asian, Native American), within the family group, or within a peer group. Crimes of abuse—sexual, verbal, etc.—are more likely to happen in the home. On the other hand, crimes of mass victimization tend to reach across primary group distinctions to touch or injure many people by depriving them of important resources for life and well-being. Such crime is likely to be perpetrated by persons and groups where wealth and resources are more heavily concentrated.

In his recent book *Good Punishment? Christian Moral Practice and U.S. Imprisonment*, James Samuel Logan cogently addresses the question of alternatives to imprisonment from a restorative justice perspective. He suggests different approaches in the development of the notion of "ontological intimacy," which he defines as "a name Christians may give to the profound human and natural interrelatedness that is rooted in a primordial communion with God." Logan continues:

> Moving beyond our reliance on counterproductive regimes of punishment toward a politics of ontological intimacy means focusing some attention on examples of practical restorative practices that move us toward addressing wrongdoing while reducing reliance on current imprisonment.[10]

Going on to deal with various systemic alternatives to prison expands the whole conversation concerning what is morally defensible in dealing with crime. Viewed against the backdrop of restorative justice as it emerged from other Christian communities, Logan's book makes a signal contribution that affords a strong resource for United Methodists seeking to engage in restorative criminal justice ministry.

4. Engaging Biblical and Theological Reflection

More than any other part of Christian heritage, Scripture's implicit concern for the importance of social context is often misunderstood or distorted. Attempts to justify failures in social holiness make it appear easier to live with ourselves; but, in reality, we're only deceiving ourselves. The responsibility to provide uplift and care for the poor, the stranger, the wounded, the lost, the homeless, and the prisoner is intrinsic to the church's calling. The idea that we are to "save souls" but avoid anything that resembles "social work" has lost any real meaning. An adequate socio-logic includes an interpretive principle that helps us see prisoners and prison systems as an important arena of God's redemptive work. The biblical warrants are clear. Thus, Bible study and theological points of view that fail to struggle with the contemporary meaning and responsibility of the church in God's work of restorative justice has little meaning or value. The will and the commitment of the church to engage the ministry in its personal and social dimensions are central expressions of faithfulness.

5. Living the Ministry and Moving to the Next Level

Last in our socio-logic of prison ministry is to craft concrete proposals for social action and social policy. While the role of the chaplain within the prison context is prescribed and thus relatively limited, there is room within this role for creative connections with families, volunteers, and community-based ministries on the outside, as well as prison administrators on the inside.

Congregational, parachurch, and community-based ministries have the most expansive opportunities to affect prison and criminal justice ministries. Opportunities to help shape restorative responses on the outside are virtually unlimited. Consider just a few: helping to sustain vital family relationships, serving as supporters and mentors for ex-offenders in reentering the community, building relationships with administrators and officers in the criminal justice system, and influencing the policy-making process. Perhaps the most important challenge is never to be satisfied with minimal accomplishment. The church's work is not done until thoroughly interactive and ongoing ministry with the incarcerated, their families, and their communities is in place and fully operational.

Conclusion

What can the church do in the midst of the issues and needs raised in this chapter? How may systematic efforts of prison and criminal justice reform be fostered in the nation, the states, and the communities? Suggestions will emerge from the chapters that follow, not in the form of complete and final remedies but rather in mapping a direction that is consistent with both constructive socio-logical and theo-logical beliefs concerning our participation in God's work of restorative justice in the world and our United Methodist ideals of sanctifying grace. In any case, if we are to be faithful, we must persevere with cooperative, holistic prison ministry of service, reform, and change toward the goal of true criminal justice in the land. By so doing, The United Methodist Church may affirm its faith, honor its heritage, and pursue its call to participate in God's work of restorative justice.

NOTES

1. See the term *logic* in the *Random House Unabridged Dictionary*, 2nd ed. (New York: Random House, 1993), 1130.

2. Warren Thomas Smith, *John Wesley and Slavery* (Nashville: Abingdon, 1986), 70, 71.

3. Marc Mauer and Ryan S. King, "Uneven Justice: State Rates of Incarceration by Race and Ethnicity." The Sentencing Project, Washington, D.C., July 2007, 1. Online at *http://www.sentencingproject.org/NewsDetails.aspx?News ID=454*.

4. Entire World—Prison Population Totals, International Centre for Prison Studies, Kings College, University of London. Online at *http://www.kcl.ac.uk/ depsta/rel/icps/worldbrief/highest_to_lowest_rates.php*.

5. China Population Information and Research Center (CPIRC). Online at *http://www.cpirc.org.cn/en/eindex.htm*; see also *http://www.kcl.ac.uk/depsta/law/ research/icps/worldbrief/wpb_stats.php?area=all&category=wb_poptotal*.

6. Tara Herivel and Paul Wright, eds., *Prison Nation: The Warehousing of America's Poor* (New York: Routledge, 2003). Section 4 (pp. 138–64) deals with the private prison industry and includes articles by Judith Greene ("Bailing Out Private Jails"), Alex Friedman ("Juvenile Crime Pays—But at What Cost?"; "University Professor Shills for Private Prison Industry"; "Juveniles Held Hostage for Profit by CSC in Florida"), and Kevin Pranis ("Campus Activism Defeats Multinational's Prison Profiteering").

7. Alan Elsner, *Gates of Injustice: The Crisis in America's Prisons* (Upper Saddle River, NJ: Financial Times Prentice Hall, 2004), 188–202.

8. Harmon L. Wray, with Peggy Hutchison, Study Guide by Brenda Connelly, *Restorative Justice: Moving Beyond Punishment* (New York: General Board of Global Ministries, The United Methodist Church, 2002), 18. Used by permission.

9. Throughout this chapter, I capitalized the term *Black* when referring to Black people, their peoplehood and institutions, and use the term interchangeably with *African American*. This is a cultural statement. The Black experience in America has been so culturally, economically, and politically demeaned, so destructively contrived as to deny the dignity and well-being of Black people. As a result, reclamation and restoration need to start at the point of identity. In the standard literary conventions of American cultures, if you are Jewish, Latino/a or Hispanic, or another ethnic group not defined solely by socially constructed ideas of race, then the common practice is to refer to you using a proper noun, capitalized, and not by modifiers that are written in lowercase letters. Since there is no intent to elevate one part of humanity above another, to capitalize the term *White* is acceptable if it is the choice of those who self-identify in that way.

10. James Samuel Logan, *Good Punishment? Christian Moral Practice and U. S. Imprisonment* (Grand Rapids, MI: Eerdmans, 2008), 201, 228.

CHAPTER 4

"Remember Those Who Are in Prison, As Though You Were in Prison with Them" (Heb. 13:3): A Biblical-Theological Mandate for Prison Ministry

JOSIAH U. YOUNG, III

If one can interpret the canon to mean that the triune Creator will leave no sinner behind—especially no *mortal* sinner—then prison chaplains have good ground to share an apocatastatic[1] interpretation with the incarcerated: All are predestined for eternal life with the triune Creator; none is predestined for "everlasting fire" or complete and utter nothingness. This would not mean that ultimate forgiveness is ethically indifferent here and now. In upholding the notion of apocatastasis, one acknowledges that sin has penultimate consequences, for the Creator never annuls justice and righteousness. It is not, then, that anything goes. Sinners (and we all are sinful) *should* repent. Still, whether an inmate is eligible for parole or not, prison ministry should convey the faith and the hope that the Creator suffered in Christ precisely to grant newness of life to the entire creation.[2] This perspective on prison ministry challenges the "theo-logic" that holds that ultimate redemption is for some rather than for all—that some people deserve damnation.[3] Which raises a question: what does one really mean by "deserve"?

One of the most troubling implications of "deserve" is the conviction that the people who inherit the worst schools and the most miserable of social existences—and who so often wind up behind bars—*warrant* their rotten fate because the Creator cannot favor them. Early American Protestants thought that African people were the cursed progeny of Ham and akin, therefore, to the Egyptians and the despised Canaanites. Although well-respected scholars have discredited that claim,[4] many people still cling to the belief that the Creator favors some and not others. I suspect that statistical analysis strengthens the claim itself in the minds of many.[5] It seems to me that as long as people believe that the Creator favors some and not others, the claim will haunt us with devastating sociological effect. If, however, an apocatastatic understanding of the canon helps divest one of such prejudice—and if a corollary of that understanding is that prison ministry ought to be devoted to redemption, healing, and justice here and now—then prison chaplains should be well equipped to challenge both the "put-down" and unjust lock-down of a people.

The Cages Must Be Dismantled

Alan Elsner points out in his book *Gates of Injustice: The Crisis in America's Prisons* that African Americans accounted for "more than 40 percent of prison and jail inmates by 2004," although Blacks "make up only 12 percent of the total U.S. population. Around one in eight African-American men in their twenties and early thirties was behind bars. The figure for Hispanics in the same age group was 4 percent; for whites, it was 1.6 percent."[6] Similarly, Professor Angela Davis, citing the 2002 Bureau of Justice Statistics in her book *Are Prisons Obsolete?*, notes: "African Americans as a whole . . . [represented] the majority of county, state, and federal prisoners, with a total of 803,400 black inmates—188,600 more than the total number of white inmates. If we include Latinos, we must add another 283,000 bodies of color."[7]

According to Elsner, the states' incarceration of Blacks began to increase around the time the civil rights movement ended and conservative politics began to rise, coincident with the assassination of Martin Luther King, Jr. For Elsner, Richard Nixon, running for president on the Republican ticket, typified such politics. After the 1968 riots, which flared in reaction to King's assassination, Elsner reports Nixon as declaring: "We need a new respect for the law in this country—a new determination that when a man disobeys the law, he pays the penalty for his crime."[8]

Who have paid the penalty? Who have been favored as the law in this country metes out the penalties? Americans use drugs in about the same proportions, says Elsner; yet Blacks, other minorities, and poor people have taken the weight of the drug legislation Congress passed. Blacks "made up 35 percent of those arrested, 55 percent of those convicted and 74 percent of those jailed for drugs possession."[9] Noam Chomsky asserts that the "so-called drug war . . . was aimed directly at the black population" and has nothing to do with drugs. "It has to do with controlling and criminalizing dangerous populations. It's kind of like a U.S. counterpart to 'social cleansing.' "[10]

Interestingly, Elsner refers to Hebrews 13:3—"remember those who are in prison as though you were in prison with them"—in his concluding chapter. Elsner quotes Supreme Court Justice Anthony Kennedy, who lamented the racial inequalities pervading the criminal justice system and the burgeoning cost involved. For Justice Kennedy, says Elsner, this reality leads to waste of resources, overly harsh punishments, and excessive prison sentences.[11] Professor Davis provides another occasion to ponder Hebrews 13:3. Through her focus on the fact that a disproportionate number of the inmates herded into the penal systems nationwide are Black and Latino, she suggests that "effective alternatives" to incarceration "involve both transformation of the techniques for addressing 'crime'" and the betterment of the socio-economic circumstances that force poor Black and Latino youth today "into the juvenile system and then on to prison." Professor Davis thus advises us to re-envision a justice system in which prisons no longer function to the detriment of people of color.[12] Davis's suggestion addresses not only the racist dimension of the criminal justice system but also the fact that prisons are inhumane institutions for too many of the incarcerated. HIV-AIDS, Hepatitis C, drug-resistant tuberculosis, and rape are all too common. The states have been incarcerating the mentally ill at an alarming rate because of the retrenchments in mental health care.[13]

Given these conditions, can we bear to remember those who are in prison as though we were in prison with them? In addition to pondering the Scriptures, prison chaplains might well consider John Edgar Wideman's advice found in his book *Brothers and Keepers:*

> The cages must be dismantled. Walls torn down. A new mass movement for human rights might begin with prison reform. Perhaps we can divert our pursuit of social justice away from punishment for some, redirect it toward entitling everybody to the basic necessities of life.[14]

The "Better" Covenant

One can argue that the biblical canon witnesses to *entitling everybody to the necessities of life* by virtue of its focus on faith and hope. One hopes that the Creator will redeem all from all the malignancies that spread injustice, disease, and death. In faith, one lives out that hope concretely through service to others. Based on this interpretation of the canon, one finds in the Bible the *primary word of grace and mercy, love, and justice.* Consider Hebrews again. "Now *faith* is the assurance of things *hoped* for, the *conviction* of things not seen" (11:1, emphasis added). And v. 3: "By faith we understand that the worlds were prepared by the word of God, so that what is seen was made from things that are not visible." Here, the *word* of God attests to the *Son* of God, who became visible in the crucified and risen Christ—in whom the Creator's love and justice have proven to be indestructible and thus eternal. Here the gospel, as the *word*—as in *rule* or *guiding* principle—clarifies and sanctifies the Hebrew Bible by placing it in an unadulterated light. We are to understand that Christ is the truest light because he is "heir of all things." The Creator, it bears repeating, has created the worlds through him. "He is the reflection of God's glory and the exact imprint of God's very being, and he sustains all things by his powerful word" (Heb. 1:2-3).

Faith and hope in his word promise that the Creator's justice and love (the two are as inextricable as faith and hope) have prevailed and are prevailing *now* in the Spirit. Moreover, faith and hope assure one, in apocalyptic fashion to be sure, that God's love and justice will vanquish injustice and enmity, which are, we are to understand, passing away: All appearances to the contrary, justice and love are prevailing. The Epistle to the Hebrews makes it clear that Christ himself is the basis of this apocalyptic hope. "Since . . . the children," meaning humankind as sons and daughters of the Creator, "share flesh and blood, [Christ] himself likewise shared the same things, so that through death he might destroy the one who has the power of death, that is, the devil, and free those who all their lives were held in slavery by the fear of death" (2:14-15). Although sinners mortified Christ, and although he succumbed to the power of death, he vanquished sin and death to bring salvation to the world. His resurrection has disclosed that it was "fitting that God, for whom and through whom all things exist, in bringing many children to glory, should make the pioneer of their salvation perfect through sufferings" (1:10). In Christ, moreover, God promises—and here certain inmates come irrepressibly to mind indeed—to remember our "sins and . . . lawlessness and . . . lawless deeds no more" (Heb. 10:17 and Jer. 31:33-34). Here, again, one holds "fast to the confession of our hope without wavering, for he who has promised is faithful" (Heb. 10:23). The matter of *covenant* is essential here.

Hebrews 8:6-7 asserts that "Jesus has now obtained a more excellent ministry, and to that degree he is the mediator of a better covenant, which has been enacted though better promises. For if that first covenant had been faultless, there would have been no need to look for a second one." The Creator initiated the "first" covenant in faithfulness to Abraham's descendants, Israel, whom the Creator has elected. Through Israel's faithfulness (and apostasy), the

Creator discloses his identity as the Supreme Being and redeemer (often wrathful) of all the nations. Like all covenants, this covenant requires reciprocity: God promises to be faithful to Israel while Israel promises to be faithful in return. From the perspective of the "better covenant," Israel's *un*faithfulness did not dissuade the Creator from sending the Son, Jesus Christ, to make the covenant good. By virtue of his true humanity, Christ is the holiest of priests (Heb. 7:11). By virtue of his true divinity, he is *the exact imprint of God's very being.* Since he embodies the two requisite dimensions sublimely, he mediates "a new covenant, so that those who are called may receive the promised eternal inheritance, because a death has occurred that redeems them from the transgressions under the first covenant" (Heb. 9:15).

Karl Barth found that "*the covenant is the internal basis of* creation," precisely because the eternal *Son*, through whom God created the world, has become *flesh* so that we may have everlasting life. Creation through the Son is thus "*intrinsically* determined as the exponent of his glory and for the *corresponding service.*"[15] "Intrinsically" signifies the preexistent Son while "corresponding service" signifies his true humanity—the faith that he has become a human being to save creation from sin and death. Based on that conception of covenant, Barth liked to preach to those who were in prison. Edified by Col. 1:19, which states "that God determined through his Son . . . 'to reconcile all things . . . unto himself,'" Barth believed that such a ministry was the only correct way to think and act canonically.[16] While he does not dismiss the view that one must take evil as seriously as the hellfire-and-brimstone preachers do, he finds that "we have no theological right to set any sort of limits to the loving-kindness of God which has appeared in Jesus Christ."[17] As Barth sees it, the church, above all, sets no limits to God's friendliness because the Creator-in-Christ hands over to the church "His witnessing and thus His affairs in the world—yes, even Himself. So great is God's loving-kindness!"[18] Surely, God embraces through the church the many thousands who have found themselves in prison. For the church, Barth writes, is "the place where the crown of humanity, namely, our" co-humanity, "may become visible in Christocentric [siblinghood]." The church is thus the place "where humanity—the humanity of God—wills to assume tangible form in time and here upon the earth."[19] Certainly, the prison ministry that denounces the sexual abuse, rampant disease, and racial and economic injustices that plague our prisons models itself on such a "tangible form."

Jürgen Moltmann finds that the *internal basis of creation* is not "the historical covenant . . . as Karl Barth maintained but 'the kingdom of glory' "[20]—"creation and covenant serve the coming kingdom."[21] He nonetheless agrees with Barth that the covenant, principally the one the Epistle to Hebrews calls the "better covenant," has its "origin" in the triune God.[22] Not unlike Barth, Moltmann makes the point that the Creator "does not encounter men and women 'as God'; he encounters them in . . . the incarnate and crucified Son."[23] Barth and Moltmann both hold that the crucified and risen One reveals who God is intrinsically and who God is in relation to the world.

Moltmann notes that the Christology one finds in Hebrews (specifically 2:16-18; 11:26; 13:13) stresses that Jesus' unjust crucifixion, his suffering, incorporates the suffering of *all* "people who suffer violence."[24] Violence does not merely refer to the enmities one person inflicts on another and that groups of people inflict on other groups. Violence characterizes all the socioeconomic contradictions that have sprung from intransigent hostilities such as racism and economic injustice. To assert that the crucified Christ incorporates the suffering of all those who are prey to violence is to proclaim, holistically, that the salvation he proffers, covenant-wise—and moreover, eschatologically—is for all. To assert that the crucified Christ incorporates the suffering of all those who are prey to violence is, in addition, to call ministers to action. If Christ's suffering *à la* Hebrews (consider 13:12-14) assures one that all will be at peace and, moreover, free and equal, *finally,* why shouldn't one work for liberty and justice for all here and now?

A Case for Faith and Hope

One can make a case for either "universal salvation" *or* "a double outcome of judgment" on the basis of Scripture as both perspectives are "well attested biblically," according to Moltmann.[25] Since the Bible upholds both positions, I cannot say the Bible offers on each of its pages a Creator who is for everyone. Consider YHWH's killing of the Egyptians' firstborn (Exod. 12:29-30); the destruction of the Canaanites (Deut. 7:1-2; Num. 21:2-3); and the chattelization of the aliens (Lev. 25:44-4). I can find no grace in YHWH's indiscriminate killing of the firstborn and read it as a shocking foreshadowing of the genocidal theology one finds in portions of Deuteronomy and Numbers. Consider what Moses, the former Egyptian, bearing the full power of YHWH's authority, tells his birth-people to do to the people of Canaan: "Utterly destroy them . . . and show no mercy to them" (Deut. 7: 1-2). Consider, too, this troubling dimension of the old covenant, in which "Israel made a vow to the Lord and said, 'If you will indeed give this people into our hands, then we will utterly destroy their towns.' The Lord listened to the voice of Israel, and handed over the Canaanites; and they utterly destroyed them and their towns" (Num. 21:2-3).

Despite what one reads in Hebrews regarding the new covenant, which perfects rather than negates the old one, it is hard to see Christ as the *exact imprint* of such a merciless God. To destroy a people, *utterly*, hardly squares with "apocatastatic" faith. As a descendent of chattel slaves, moreover, I find Lev. 25:44-46 troubling. The entire chapter is about YHWH's instructions to Moses regarding the jubilees that are to take place every fifty years. The instructions carry the unimpeachable authority of the burning bush and its troubling association with the conquest: "I am the LORD your God, who brought you out of the land of Egypt, to give you the land of Canaan, to be your God" (Lev. 25:38). The Lord tells Moses that the Hebrews who will fall on hard times and so into indentured servitude are to be released at the half-century mark. Such servants, after all, belong to YHWH, as he "brought [them] out of the land of Egypt"; hence *they* "shall not be sold as slaves are sold" and are not to be treated harshly (Lev. 25:42). YHWH tells Moses that his people may enslave the foreigners: "You may also acquire . . . the aliens residing with you, and from their families that are with you, who have been born in your land; and they may be your property. You may keep them as a possession for your children after you, for them to inherit as property. These you may treat as slaves, but as for your fellow Israelites, no one shall rule over the other with harshness" (Lev. 25:45-46). The non-Hebrew slaves—the *aliens* YHWH's people acquired along the way—have no (jubilee) rights.

A Creator Who Is No Respecter of Persons?

What are we to make of the Creator's disdain for the aliens, the non-favored others? Does the canon compel us to see its contradictions so that we can stake our faith and hope on who we believe the Creator *truly* is, and in the spirit of who we are, truly, today? Whatever the reasons, the Bible's contradictions are hardly passé. They are, in fact, very timely. They bring to mind those who are in prison, in part, because many of us, until today, have not yet freed ourselves from brutally exclusive ways of construing election.

In an essay entitled "Color Bind: Prisons and the New American Racism," Paul Street, the director of research at the Urban League of Chicago, writes, "[The] Justice Policy Institute [of New York State] reports that in the 1990s more blacks entered prison just for drug offenses than graduated from the state's massive university system with undergraduate, masters, and doctoral degrees combined."[26] He asks: "Do the cheerleaders of 'get tough' crime and sentencing policy really believe that African Americans deserve to suffer so disproportionately at the hands of the criminal justice system?"[27] I think that many really *do* believe that, and precisely for the reasons I have just discussed. In ghettoizing and criminalizing African Americans and other allegedly non-elect people, in perpetuating such violence on them, the society makes it nearly impossible for a good number of us to escape what appears to be its goal: incarceration. If the Bible itself proffers a viable alternative to such an end, then perhaps it would be wise to adopt the apocatastatic perspective, especially, here, for the sake of those in prison.

I have no choice *but* to remember them as though I were in prison with them for I surely *could* have been.[28] I grew up in one of New York City's Black and Latino ghettos and saw many of my peers succumb to an early grave or to the penal system. I am fortunate to have both passed the half-century mark and escaped the clutches of the system. I am no better, really, than my counterparts who were far less fortunate. I, then, do not feel that the Creator smiled on me but frowned on them. We were all in the same hold, really. The only difference among us was that the horror of those mean streets frightened and infuriated me (as I am sure that it did them)—to such a point that I refused to think that we, all of us, were nothing but prison fodder. How I made good on that refusal has to do with a rather mysterious calling: I became a theologian—political and apocatastatic—to try to be a witness to a loving and just Creator, partly for the sakes of my brothers and sisters in prison. I have the hope and the faith that more and more people in and of the churches will view them as siblings too—will remember them, and serve them for the sake of the friendly Creator, for the sake of freedom and justice for all, for the sake of a new creation that is "no respecter of persons."

There are no theologies and no takes on our ultimate salvation that are value-free—especially regarding the *political* decisions we make as to *who* goes to prison and what their fates are once they wind up there. I, for one, see no really good reason to use Scripture or the history of Christian thought to buttress, however subliminally, the view that the African Americans and the Latinos who are incarcerated at a rate disproportionate to their numbers have been *predestined* to endure such a fate, as if their lock-ups attest provisionally to their unworthiness for eternal life. I see no good reason to think that about *any* of the incarcerated. With the Bible's help, and that of certain highly influential theologians, why not envision a God-in-Christ who will save all of us? Why not undertake prison reform and the revision of our social policies accordingly?

NOTES

1. "Apocatatasic" (from *apocatastasis* or *apokatastasis*) means the universal restoration of all things, as suggested by Col. 1:19–20.

2. As an example of this perspective, see Jürgen Moltmann, *The Coming of God* (Minneapolis: Fortress, 2004), 245.

3. Consider what Augustine—the ancient, but still influential theologian—had to say against the proposition that the Creator will save all. See, for example, his *City of God*, XXI:23.

4. See, as examples, David Goldenberg, *The Curse of Ham: Race and Slavery in Early Judaism, Christianity and Islam* (Princeton, NJ: Princeton University Press, 2003); Stephen Haynes, *Noah's Curse: The Biblical Justification of American Slavery* (New York: Oxford University Press, 2002); Regina Schwartz, *The Curse of Cain: The Violent Legacy of Monotheism* (Chicago: The University of Chicago, 1997).

5. This is not to suggest that African Americans have symbolized the cursed sinner alone. We are, at bottom, invested with ambivalence that bears, heuristically it seems to me, an affinity to the ambivalence one finds in the Bible itself—principally, here, the difference between apocatastasis and double predestination. Essayist Ralph Ellison has greatly influenced my point of view. See his "Perspective of Literature," in *The Collected Essays of Ralph Ellison*, edited by John F. Callahan (New York: The Modern Library, 1995), 778–79, in which he argues that race has become "a major cause, form and symbol of the American hierarchical psychosis. . . . [The] Afro-American . . . was to be viewed, at least by many whites, as both cause and cure of our social malaise." Even so, the negative association concerns me now. The high ratio of Black men and women in prison reveals a deep and eminently historical bias against them. It would be unreasonable to suppose that the Bible—as formative as it has been in shaping the North American ethos—has not played a role in our problematic imprisonment.

6. Alan Elsner, *Gates of Injustice: The Crisis in America's Prisons*, 1st Edition, © Pgs. 13, 18, 21. Reprinted by permission of Pearson Education, Inc., Upper Saddle River, NJ.

7. Angela Davis, *Are Prisons Obsolete?* (New York: Seven Stories Press, 2003), 94. Used by permission.

8. Elsner, *Gates of Injustice*, 18.

9. Ibid., 21. "Since African Americans account for about one eighth of the population, one would expect them to account for a similar proportion of drugs-related arrests, all other things being equal. However, statistics show a lopsided arrest, conviction, and incarceration rate for African Americans."

10. Noam Chomsky, "Drug Policy as Social Control," in *Prison Nation: The Warehousing of America's Poor*, edited by Tara Herivel and Paul Wright (New York: Routledge, 2003), 58. Used by permission.

11. Elsner, *Gates of Injustice*, 232–33.

12. Davis, *Are Prisons Obsolete?* 21.

13. See Herivel and Wright, *Prison Nation*; Elsner, *Gates of Injustice*; and Davis, *Are Prisons Obsolete?*

14. John Edgar Wideman, *Brothers and Keepers* (New York: Houghton Mifflin, 2005), xvii. Wideman, a professor of Africana Studies at Brown University, is an

award-winning novelist. *Brothers and Keepers,* a work of nonfiction, was a finalist for the National Book Award and is about his brother Robert (Robby) Wideman, who is serving a life term in one of our nation's prisons.

15. Karl Barth, "Creation and Covenant" (*Church Dogmatics,* III/1, 230–32), in *Karl Barth: Theologian of Freedom,* ed. Clifford Green (London: Collins Publisher, 1989), 190–91, emphases added.

16. Karl Barth, The *Humanity of God* (Louisville: Westminster/John Knox Press, 1960), 61.

17. Ibid., 62.

18. Ibid., 64.

19. Ibid., 65.

20. Jürgen Moltmann, *God in Creation: A New Theology of Creation and the Spirit of God* (Minneapolis: Fortress, 1993), 55.

21. Ibid., 329 (fn).

22. Jürgen Moltmann, *The Trinity and the Kingdom: The Doctrine of God* (Minneapolis: Fortress, 1993), 58.

23. Ibid., 119.

24. Moltmann, *The Spirit of Life: A Universal Affirmation* (Minneapolis: Fortress, 2001), 130–31.

25. Moltmann, *The Coming of God,* 241.

26. Paul Street, "Color Bind: Prisons and the New American Racism," in *Prison Nation,* 32.

27. Ibid., 37.

28. For a corroborating witness to what I'm talking about, see Wideman's *Brothers and Keepers.*

Section 3

Historical
Perspectives

CHAPTER 5

Prison Ministry in the Wesleyan Heritage

RICHARD P. HEITZENRATER

Engagement in prison ministry has been a defining feature of Methodism from the very beginning of the Wesleyan heritage. While a tutor at Oxford University in the early eighteenth century, John Wesley began to implement his mission of holy living within the larger community. He saw the necessity of combining a pattern of intense personal piety with a program of practical social concern—a scriptural and practical combination of works of piety and works of mercy that he felt was crucial for a person to exhibit both love of God and love of neighbor, the heart of the Christian faith.

John Wesley's personal approach to "holy living," which accompanied his preparation for taking holy orders in 1725, soon began to take on more corporate and social dimensions as his brother Charles and others joined with him in this endeavor to lead a vital Christian life. They were not, of course, the first to visit the prisons, much less care for the poor, more broadly speaking. But their activities came at an important juncture, as the British penal system became more harsh and as the reaction against its cruelty and injustice began to grow.

British Justice and Eighteenth-Century Methodism

The criminal justice system was quite different in Wesley's day from what it is today. The penal code in England during the eighteenth century was very severe. More than half of the trials generally resulted in conviction, and the penalty for a large percentage of the crimes was death by hanging.[1] A regulation passed at mid-century required that the execution take place within forty-eight hours. There were no prisoners spending countless days in prison on death row.

Prisoners, in general, were not incarcerated for long periods of time.[2] Except for debtors, who were held until they could pay their debts (a real conundrum), most prisoners were either held a short time for execution, which was generally a public hanging, or were given sentences that entailed a set period of public ridicule and torture, such as being burned in the hand or pilloried in the stocks. The public nature of punishment, on the theory that such display would be a deterrent to crime, was such that the dead bodies of those who had committed suicide (which was considered to be a crime as well as a sin) were hung from public galleries for all to see.

Many of the crimes that sent people to prison were property crimes—theft, burglary, larceny. Many of these were petty crimes; but in a land with a growing propertied class and an increasing number of poor people, these crimes were seen as crimes against persons, especially if the property were stolen off the person. And crime began to be associated more and more with the lower classes, linked to the poor, even if they were not necessarily a criminal class. Crime was crime; and, in many instances, the differentiation of punishment between murder and stealing a handkerchief from a back pocket was not that great.

There were several impediments to prison visitation. The shortness of the incarceration meant that many prisoners were executed before they received any ministration.[3] The overcrowded living conditions in the prisons were poor—there was not only a dearth of cleanliness, food, clothing, and proper care but also a prevalence of disease and disruption. Jail fever and other illnesses took their toll, to the extent that in some periods more prisoners died from disease than from execution. Simply being imprisoned could, therefore, mean a death sentence. Prisoners were mixed—sick and well, young and old, hardened and novice criminals. Persons imprisoned for debt had little means of earning their ransom, except for the regulation that allowed them (and the keepers) to sell beer to the other prisoners.

Many people did not worry about such conditions but saw the suffering of the prisoners as part of their punishment. They had broken God's laws and did not deserve any better. The justice system was viewed not as a means of rehabilitation but of punishment. Public hangings were meant to serve as deterrents to crime but, more often than not, simply provided public entertainment. The chaplains ("ordinaries") and wardens were mainly charged with maintaining the peace within the institutions. In many cases, this meant doing whatever was minimally necessary to prevent disruptions and disorder, rather than doing much that could be considered positive work with the prisoners. The ministers who preached the Assize Sermons at the beginning of the quarterly court sessions usually said a few words to support the work of the magistrates as agents of God.[4]

Under these circumstances, very few people took the time or made the effort to visit the prisons. In most people's minds, the prisoners were simply receiving their just punishment for breaking the law. The public chose to turn a blind eye to the inequities of the law, the conditions of the prisons, and the implicit blight that such a situation presented to their social order.

Prison Visitation in Oxford Methodism

The public apathy toward the plight of prisoners did not deter the Wesleys and their friends at Oxford from visiting the city jail and the county prison. Their corporate pattern of study and devotion began among a small group of only three or four university men in 1729 but soon branched out into a program of social outreach. William Morgan stopped by the county prison at the Castle one day in the summer of 1730 to see a man who had been convicted of killing his wife. A conversation with another prisoner, incarcerated for debt, convinced him that "it would do much good if anyone would be at the pains of now and then speaking with them."[5] Morgan nagged the Wesleys so much that in August, John and Charles walked with him to the Castle Prison. They were so pleased with the results that they agreed to visit the prisoners once or twice a week from thenceforward. Before the year was out, they also began visiting the city jail at the north gate, Bocardo.[6] Thus began their program of outreach, which soon broadened to include visiting the sick, teaching the poor children, feeding the hungry, and reaching out to the needy in the city.

Their design and method were spelled out in a list of questions that Wesley drew up, based on the premise: "Whether we can be happy at all hereafter, unless we have, according to our power, 'fed the hungry, clothed the naked, visited those that are sick or in prison'; and make all these actions subservient to an higher purpose, even the saving of souls from death?" The questions they proposed to others, especially their opponents, included: "Whether . . . we may not try to do good to those that are in prison? In particular, whether we may not release such well-disposed persons as remain in prison for small sums?" Wesley also noted their intent to help those who need it the most, by giving them clothes, medicine, Bibles, and devotional books, along with preaching, praying, and presiding over the Sacrament.[7] This program developed to the point where one of the group visited each of the prisons, Castle and Bocardo, every day to talk, read, and pray with the prisoners, instruct them in Christian practices, conduct the Prayer Service on Wednesdays and Fridays, and preside over the Eucharist every Sunday.[8]

The public then began to take notice of this small group that was trying to exercise vital Christian living in their community, which brought the weight of public ridicule upon them. Over the next few months in 1730–31, their detractors gave the Wesleyan group a succession of sarcastic names like the Godly Club, the Holy Club, and Supererogation Men—all of which were superseded in mid-1732 by "Methodists," a term that had been used against the English Arminians of the previous generation for using a "new method" in theology.[9] In the same letter in which John Clayton mentioned to

John Wesley that the group had garnered the name "Methodist," he also noted their satisfaction that some of the accused felons in the prison had been acquitted.[10] Clayton also informed Wesley that they were convinced of the innocence of one very unpopular prisoner accused of sodomy, John Blair; and Wesley proceeded to assist in his defense by drawing up a legal brief for Blair and attending his trial in Thame, where the accused was found not guilty.[11]

In most cases, however, the Wesleys and their followers were more interested in helping free the convicted prisoners from sin and spiritual death than in freeing them from their sentence and imprisonment.[12] At Oxford in 1734, Wesley recorded in his diary that, over the period of more than a week, he had religious talk and prayed with Edward Pope, a condemned prisoner in the Castle, including a conversation just before the man was executed, during which he did not confess to stealing a colt, the charge against him. Wesley apparently watched the hanging and waited until they brought the body back into the prison. At their regular meeting that evening, the Methodists talked about their work at the Castle, and particularly about Pope, before they considered the matter of holiness by reading William Law's book on Christian perfection.[13] Such experiences no doubt made a strong impression on those young men as they searched for a true sense of the Christian life and strove to implement it in their minds, hearts, and lives. Both Charles and John recount visiting many condemned prisoners, praying with them in their cells, accompanying them to the gallows, and helping them approach death with penitent hearts and calm spirits.

This approach represented their best understanding of what the Lord required of them in those circumstances. Their historical context did not provide the perspective from which to judge the penal system as generally inadequate—that task of reform arose in the following century. In their own time, they did nevertheless help many prisoners escape their debts; alleviate the physical needs of many inmates; assist the families of many convicts; and comfort and assure many condemned men on their way to the gallows. Their "reforms" in the prisons were primarily confined to the reformation and transformation of many prisoners. In those tasks, they were following their understanding of what it meant to imitate the life of Christ and walk as he walked.

Developing the Work in the Prisons

The prison work at Oxford continued even when the Wesleys went to Georgia. Richard Morgan, Jr., visited the Bocardo several days a week in the ensuing years. George Whitefield also visited in the prisons during that time. When Charles Wesley returned from Georgia, he renewed the Methodists' work in the prisons, expanding the scope to include Newgate and Marshalsea prisons in London, Newgate prison in Bristol, and Cardiff prison in Wales. When John returned, he once again joined in the work with the prisoners, even riding with the condemned to their execution at Tyburn, as he records in his diary:

> November 8, 1738. . . . 6.30 Newgate with Charles, all believed. 7 Communion, read Prayers, preached. 9 In the coach, meditated, sang. 10 At St. Giles', tea. 10.30 Tyburn; meditated. 11 In the cart, prayed. 12 Sang, prayed, all cheerful. 12 They died; prayed. 1 Preached to the mob.[14]

Two years after John returned from Georgia, and nearly a year and a half after his Aldersgate experience, Wesley went back to Oxford and bemoaned the "shattered condition" of the work there: "The poor prisoners both in the Castle and in the City Prison had now none that cared for their souls, none to instruct, advise, comfort, and build them up in the knowledge and love of the Lord Jesus. None left to visit the workhouses, where also we used to meet with the most moving objects of compassion."[15]

In the next few years, the Wesleys introduced a number of friends and followers to the prison ministry, such as Sarah Peters[16] and Silas Told, whose journal includes an account of his work.[17] And Wesley became a close friend and supporter of John Howard, one of the first prison reformers in Great Britain.[18]

Wesley's approach was very practical and entailed getting many people involved in the work. For instance, in November 1759, when he discovered that the French prisoners at Knowle were approaching the cold winter without adequate clothing, he collected twenty-three pounds (more than $2,000 today) at the New Room, Bristol, and dispersed it as follows:

> Judged it best to lay this out in shirts and flannel waistcoats, and accordingly bought, of Mr. Zepheniah Fry, in the Castle, check shirts and woollen cloth to the amount of £8 10s. 6d.; and of Mrs. Sarah Cole, check linen to the amount of £5 17s. The linen was immediately delivered to two or three poor women, who were to be paid the common price, and to some others, who offered to make them into shirts, etc., for nothing. The money remaining I lodged in the hands of Mr. James Ireland of Horsleydown Street, as he speaks French readily, and Mr. John Salter of Bedminster, who had been with me both at the prison and the hospital. I directed them to give a waistcoat and two shirts to every one who was remanded from the hospital to the prison, and the other half to those they should judge most needy or most deserving.[19]

However, a year later he discovered that the French prisoners there were once again suffering from lack of clothing, in spite of the Methodists' efforts the previous fall. He made yet another collection and sent the money "to be laid out in linen and waistcoats, which were given to those that were most in want."[20]

Wesley also reveals how he dispensed these funds in a letter to the editor of *Lloyd's Evening Post* in February 1760, describing what good work in the prisons a twenty-pound note could support:

> I received a £20 Bank bill from an anonymous correspondent, who desired me to lay it out in the manner I judged best for the use of poor prisoners. I immediately employed some in whom I could confide to inquire into the circumstances of those confined in Whitechapel and New Prison. I knew the former to have very little allowance even of bread, and the latter none at all. Upon inquiry they found one poor woman in Whitechapel Prison very big with child and destitute of all things. At the

same time I casually heard of a poor man who had been confined for nine months in the Poultry Compter, while his wife and three children (whom he before maintained by his labour) were almost perishing through want. Not long after, another poor woman, who had been diligent in helping others, was herself thrown into Whitechapel Prison. The expense of discharging these three and giving them a few necessaries amounted to £10 10s. One pound fourteen shillings I expended in stockings and other clothing, which was given to those prisoners who were in the most pressing want. The remainder, £7 16s., was laid out in bread, which was warily distributed thrice a week. I am therefore assured that the whole of this sum was laid out in real charity. And how much more noble a satisfaction must result from this to the generous benefactor . . . than he could receive from an embroidered suit of clothes or a piece of plate made in the newest fashion! Men of reason, judge![21]

In his attempts to keep the public informed of the Methodists' reasons for visiting the prisons and the conditions they met in such places, Wesley sent several other letters to the periodical publications of his day. By describing the improvement in the conditions in Newgate Prison, Bristol, in 1761, he implicitly lifts up the dire state of the former conditions:

Of all the seats of woe on this side hell few, I suppose, exceed or even equal Newgate. If any region of horror could exceed it a few years ago, Newgate in Bristol did; so great was the filth, the stench, the misery, and wickedness which shocked all who had a spark of humanity left. How was I surprised, then, when I was there a few weeks ago! (1) Every part of it . . . is as clean and sweet as a gentleman's house; . . . (2) Here is no fighting or brawling . . . (3) The usual grounds of quarrelling are removed; . . . (4) Here is no drunkenness suffered, . . . (5) Nor any whoredom, the women prisoners being narrowly observed and kept separate from the men; . . . (6) All possible care is taken to prevent idleness: . . . . (7) Only on the Lord's Day they neither work nor play, but dress themselves as clean as they can, to attend the public service in the chapel . . . (8) . . . Besides a sermon every Sunday and Thursday, they have a large Bible chained on one side of the chapel, . . . By the blessing of God on these regulations the prison now has a new face: nothing offends either the eye or ear; and the whole has the appearance of a quiet, serious family.[22]

He similarly portrayed the improved conditions at the Knowle prison in somewhat glowing terms in the fall of 1759 in a letter to *Lloyd's Evening Post.*[23]

Evangelism in the Prison Work

The public display of criminals did not deter the Methodists from ministering to those in need. Hogarth's famous painting of a criminal being transported by cart to be hanged at Tyburn shows a Methodist preacher in the cart with the prisoner, faithfully reading one of Wesley's sermons to the condemned man. The power of what they said in such circumstances is evident in Wesley's little tract "A Word to a Condemned Malefactor." In the four-page pamphlet, he minces no words in the very straightforward picture he paints of the plight of the prisoner, who could possibly even hear the gallows being prepared for his immanent doom:

> What a condition are you in! The sentence is passed; you are condemned to die; and this sentence is to be executed shortly! You have no way to escape; these fetters, these walls, these gates and bars, these keepers, cut off all hope: Therefore, die you must. But must you die like a beast, without thinking what it is to die? You need not; you will not; you will think a little first; you will consider, "What is death?"

Wesley then leads the prisoner through the apparent despair of his condition—his lack of true holiness, or "having the mind that was in Christ"—to the aspirant hope for eternity, if he will only repent and believe. People frequently are surprised at Wesley's published sermons because they often have no evangelical appeal at the end, no plea for change, no call for decision. But this little tract rises to a powerful climax in the last few sentences:

> Believe in Christ, as your Lord and your God, your wisdom and righteousness, sanctification and redemption. Believe in him with your whole heart. Cast your whole soul upon his love. Trust Him alone; love Him alone; fear Him alone; and cleave to Him alone; till He shall say to you (as to the dying malefactor of old), "This day shalt thou be with me in paradise."[24]

These strong words to the condemned prisoner awaiting execution in the jail also provide the framework and power behind the imagery that Charles Wesley uses for every person bound by the chains of sin, as evident in these powerful lines from his sermon, "Awake, Thou that Sleepest":

> Thou unholy soul, see thy picture in condemned Peter, lying in the dark dungeon, between the soldiers, bound with two chains, the keepers before the door keeping the prison. The night is far spent, the morning is at hand, when thou art to be brought forth to execution. And in these dreadful circumstances, thou art fast asleep; thou art fast asleep in the devil's arms, on the brink of the pit, in the jaws of everlasting destruction![25]

To "do much good," including such activities as visiting those in prison, became such a distinctive expectation of the Methodists and fit so well into their whole scheme of doctrine and discipline that it was spelled out as one of the three General Rules that were necessary to follow in order to remain a member of the United Societies of the People Called Methodists.[26] Although Wesley never felt that these "rules" (doing good, avoiding evil, using the means of grace) encompassed the totality of what it means to be a Christian, he rather consistently felt that one could not claim to be truly desiring of salvation unless these three marks were consistently present in a person's life.

Wesley's diary for that period mentions and outlines their "method" of proceeding at the Castle prison (for county prisoners) and the Bocardo jail (for city prisoners). This practical method outlined the rotation for visitation (who would visit on what days) and the activities that would mark their visits: distributing books and food; talking with individuals; preaching to groups; contacting the families; and communicating with the chaplains and wardens.

Rationale and Motivation for Prison Work

The Wesleyan program had not only a practical method of proceeding but also developed upon a specifically theological method. The theological method developed upon scriptural grounds, interpreted from their basically Arminian perspective.

Scriptural

The Oxford Methodist method of visiting prisoners was based on two scriptural citations: the injunction of Jesus that we should love God and love our neighbor (the "Great Commandment" in Matt. 22:37-39) and the teaching of Jesus that when we love our neighbor, we love God (Matt. 25:35-40). The life of Christ was the model of holy living that Wesley and the Methodists strove to follow; and the power of the Holy Spirit provided the energy for their dual program of vital devotion to God and active involvement in helping the needs of their neighbors. These two passages provided the basic rationale for their approach to the religious life, which focused both on works of piety and on works of mercy in response to God's transforming power in their lives. John Wesley summarized the relationship between the two passages in one of his sermons: "As the love of God naturally leads to works of piety, so the love of our neighbour naturally leads all that feel it to works of mercy. It inclines us to feed the hungry, to clothe the naked, to visit them that are sick or in prison. . . ."[27]

Theological

The "holy living" tradition that informed and motivated Wesley was not based on "works righteousness" or on earning one's salvation by doing good works, as is often claimed (especially by Moravians and Calvinists in his day as well as some Methodists later). Rather, it was part of an approach to vital Christian living that was grounded in Scripture and might better be called "meditative piety," which relies in part on a virtue ethic. The point was not so much to "do" what was *right* and "not do" what was *wrong* (simply an obedience ethic), or even to have some scale of what was better or worse (a value ethic). Rather their approach was grounded in the assumption that what one *does* derives from who one *is—being* precedes *doing*.[28]

From such a perspective, the point is to become like the model of virtue that informs one's understanding of the good, of proper humanity. For the Christian, that means one should strive to be like Christ (*imitatio Christi*). Meditation and prayer were aimed at opening oneself to the presence and power of God working in one's life (i.e., grace) in such a way as to be filled by the biblical virtues, seen in the life of Christ. These virtues would thus flush out the sinful vices—love instead of hate, humility instead of pride, thankfulness instead of greed, and so forth. This perspective is what motivated Wesley and many others in the holy living tradition; and this approach fit well into his lifelong brand of Arminian theology and soteriology.

Historical

John Wesley's practice of prison visitation was also built on a historical precedent established by his predecessors, including his father and brother. When Samuel discovered that his son was interested in visiting the prisons in 1730, he sent an encouraging letter, pointing out that he also had visited the Castle prison when he was a student at Oxford, "and reflect on it with great satisfaction to this day."[29]

The previous year, John had read a poem by his brother, Samuel, entitled, "The Prisons Open'd," which praised the work of an investigating committee of the House of Commons, chaired by Colonel James Oglethorpe.[30] The public attitude toward the despicable state of the prisons shines through Samuel's poetry:

Conscious of ill-us'd pow'r, and public hate,
Then other tyrants fear'd approaching fate;
An universal groan the prisons gave,
And Newgate trembled thro' her inmost cave,
Lest farther searches farther crimes reveal,
Which arts infernal labour to conceal;
Lest pity's eye those regions should explore,
Where beams of mercy never reach'd before,
Unwelcome light on darkest dungeons throw,
And ev'ry latent depth of horror show.[31]

Oglethorpe's interest in the prisons had been spurred by the death in prison of a writer-friend (imprisoned for debt) who had been purposely exposed to small pox by a malicious warden. His growing knowledge of the problem of debtors in prison spurred him to found the colony of Georgia to provide an opportunity for some of the victims of the system.

Of course, the historical precedents for Christians visiting the prisons were nearly as old as Christianity itself. Wesley was well aware of the work of the apostles and the early church, who also took the life and work of Jesus as their model and tried to implement his teachings in their own lives.

Practical

The Methodists' work among the working class of England has often been seen as a crucial, if conservative, element in keeping the working class from rising up against the establishment, as was happening in some other countries in the eighteenth century, such as France. Certainly, Wesley was concerned about the public order, since the Methodists were often the brunt of social disorders, mobs, and riots. More important, however, he viewed the practical plight of the marginalized classes in England with a nascent social consciousness that recognized the role of government and institutions in both causing and solving the problems.

England had never experienced the kind of poverty and social upheaval that had marked some other parts of Europe. Although Wesley reacted negatively to Adam Smith's support for surplus accumulation as a key element in increasing the wealth and strength of the nation, Wesley shared the view that things could be relatively better, that all people should have the opportunity to flourish, and that everyone—rich or poor—should or could have a role in contributing to the well-being of society. He was a proud Englishman and never completely escaped the practical elements that fed such national pride. One might say this approach did have revolutionary potential within the divisive social stratification in his day. But Wesley's view, thoroughly practical in one sense, was always undergirded by a scriptural and theological rationale that made every Christian activity a response to the triune God working in and through one's life.

Prison Ministry and the Christian Vocation

Charles Wesley summarizes the relationship between service, obedience, and vocation in one couplet from a familiar hymn: "To serve the present age, my calling to fulfill. / O, may it all my powers engage, to do my Master's will." Doing the Master's will, for the Wesleys, meant above all fulfilling the Great Commandment—to love your God and to love your neighbor. And loving God necessarily entailed not only works of piety and devotion, such as worship, prayer, Scripture reading, and religious conversation. Loving God also entailed works of mercy through love of neighbor.

As a Service to God

Prison ministry is a service to God as seen in the picture of the judgment day in Matthew 25 and parallel passages. Wesley says that this story, the third in a row in that chapter, shows that there is no "negative goodness."[32] Spirituality does not consist primarily in the refraining from doing things that might be considered sinful. Sin can consist, however, in refraining from doing good. Our Lord insists that a person truly loves God only when he or she demonstrates that love to neighbor: feeding the hungry, clothing the naked, visiting the sick and the prisoners—"Inasmuch as you did it to one of the least of these my brethren, you did it unto me."[33] The two commands, to love God and to neighbor, were inextricably linked as one. To love and serve God was to love and serve neighbor.

As Love of Neighbor

The second half of the Great Commandment, the core of the Wesleyan message, is "You shall love your neighbor as yourself" (Matt. 22:39). Love of neighbor is neither an abstract concept nor a misdirected egoism. Wesley makes this clear when he explains the rationale for visiting prisoners. He reminds his people that a prisoner is one of us, part of the family of God. He develops a deeply empathetic concept of loving your neighbor "as yourself" when he comments on Heb. 13:3 in his *Explanatory Notes Upon the New Testament:* "Remember in your prayers and by your help, 'them that are in bonds, as being bound with them'—seeing ye are members one of another."[34]

This broadening of the family of God to incorporate the sick, the prisoners, the poor, the children—the disenfranchised members of society—is one of the great lessons that Wesley learned from Scripture and tried to apply within Methodism. His active program of medical clinics, subsidized housing, educational institutions, money lending, visiting the sick—all of these "works of mercy" were aimed, as he often said, especially "for those of the family of faith" (Gal. 6:10). But this was not necessarily a closed institutional view, since his Arminian view of universal atonement meant that everyone was a child of God, in one sense, and potentially a person of faith as well. Therefore, he could visit the prison cells without checking first to see if the prisoner was a Methodist. Everyone under those circumstances stood in need of God's power and love. Jesus made that point very clearly in his parable of the Good Samaritan, which Wesley again summarizes in the *Explanatory Notes.* Bigotry and party zeal, he reminds us, "contracts our hearts" and makes us love only those who are like us so that our love to them "is but self-love reflected."

This narrowness is not what Jesus was talking about when he said to love our neighbor as ourselves. Instead, if we have an honest openness of mind, we will remember the kinship among all humankind, and "cultivate that happy instinct whereby in the original constitution of our nature, God has strongly bound us to each other."[35]

As a Work of Mercy

Following the Great Commandment to love God and neighbor means that we should do both works of piety and works of mercy. But Wesley reverses the priorities assumed by many Christians that works of piety are our primary task. In his sermon "On Zeal" he points out that one should be zealous for the church and certainly not neglect any of the ordinances of God, but he goes on to say very explicitly:

> But are you more zealous for 'works of mercy' than even for works of piety? Do *you* follow the example of your Lord, and prefer mercy even before sacrifice? Do you use all diligence in feeding the hungry, clothing the naked, visiting them that are sick and in prison?[36]

This view of the primary place for works of mercy in the Christian life is reinforced throughout this sermon, where Wesley places such works on an equal plane with works of piety as means of grace.

As a "Plain Duty"

Just as in the words of Jesus, Wesley also links visiting the sick and the prisoners. His sermon "On Visiting the Sick" could, therefore, also be seen as a guide for his views on visiting prisoners. He provides there not only the scriptural injunctions and the nature of this "plain duty" (as he calls it), but also a detailed method of how to proceed and a rationale for participation in such a program by all segments of society, including women. He even argues that the poor should visit the poor, quoting a hymn by Isaac Watts that he had included in his first collection of *Psalms and Hymns* in 1737:

Go on! Thou poor disciple of a poor Master! Do as he did in the days of his flesh! Whenever thou hast an opportunity, go about doing good, and healing all that are oppressed of the devil; encouraging them to shake off his chains, and fly immediately to him

> Who sets the prisoners free, and breaks
> The iron bondage from their necks.[37]

For Wesley, Jesus' point about visiting those who are sick or in prison is not just a matter of giving more money for home missions or of supporting programs that help those under such burdens. Wesley would call it "a plain duty" that we, in fact, *do* the visiting. And he very clearly points out that to "visit," speaking etymologically, means "to look upon" the person with your own eyes.[38] Otherwise, we do not really know what the poor, the sick, and the imprisoned are suffering. Many of us have a "voluntary ignorance" of such matters, since we have no contact with them. Many of us "do not care to know"—we avoid such knowledge by steering clear of any first-hand knowledge or involvement, and then use our ignorance as an excuse for inaction, if not hardness of heart. We pass by "on the other side," looking at the sky, reading a book, or listening to the birds in the trees rather than paying attention to the suffering practically under our feet.[39]

One of the major implications of such indirection—leaving it to someone else, even if we contribute to their support (e.g., a doctor or chaplain)—is not only that we fail to fulfill our duty to visit those in prison but also that we do not receive the same benefit than if we see the prisoner with our own eyes. If you do not fulfill your "plain duty" by visiting, as Wesley points out, you "lose a means of grace."[40]

As a Covered Promise

Such obligations, however, are not simply divine commands that leave Christians struggling with their own initiative and strength, which they are often hesitant to do. An important principle for Wesley was that any divine command is a "covered promise": If God asks you to do something, God will assist you to do it; God will empower you to act. Wesley spells out this principle in Sermon 25:

> Every command in Holy Writ is only a covered promise. For by that solemn declaration, 'This is the covenant I will make after those days, saith the Lord; I will put my laws in your minds, and write them in your hearts,' [Heb. 10:10] God hath engaged to give whatsoever he commands. Does he command us then to 'pray without ceasing'? To 'rejoice evermore'? To be 'holy as he is holy'? [1 Thess. 5:16-17; 1 Peter 1:16]. It is enough. He will work in us this very thing. It shall be unto us according to his word.[41]

Therefore, in Wesley's view, the plain duty of visiting the prisoners also presents an occasion for God to assist us as we attempt to fulfill our obligation to do God's will. To use Wesleyan theological language, visiting the prisons can therefore be a means of grace.

As a Means of Grace

One of the most important contributions of Wesleyan theology to the body of Christian theology is his enlivened concept of "grace" and his broadened view of the "means of grace." The beginning of his sermon "On Visiting the Sick" explains his view rather unambiguously:

> It is generally supposed that 'the means of grace' and 'the ordinances of God' are equivalent terms. We usually mean by that expression those that are usually termed 'works of piety,' namely, hearing and reading the Scripture, receiving the Lord's Supper, public and private prayer, and fasting. And it is certain these are the ordinary channels which convey the grace of God to the souls of men. But are they the only means of grace? Are there no other means than these whereby God is pleased, frequently, yea, ordinarily to convey his grace to them that either love or fear him? Surely there are works of mercy, as well as works of piety, which are real means of grace. They are more especially such to those that perform them with a single eye.

And those that neglect them do not receive the grace which otherwise they might.[42]

To understand fully the importance of what Wesley is saying here, we must know what he means by *grace* and then what the implications are for the concept of *means of grace*, which he has redefined for most Christians.

Wesley sometimes uses the term *grace* to mean the traditional Christian view of God's unmerited mercy—the divine attitude toward us from which springs God's willingness to act toward us in ways we do not deserve, such as in pardoning us from our sins (justification). But generally Wesley's view of grace entails the more active relational concept of God's power and presence in our lives, transforming us through the work of the Holy Spirit (often related to sanctification).

But in this place[43] it rather means that power of God the Holy Ghost which 'worketh in us both to will and to do of his good pleasure.' As soon as ever the grace of God (in the former sense, his pardoning love) is manifested to our soul, the grace of God (in the latter sense, the power of his Spirit) takes place therein. And now we can perform, through God, what to man was impossible.[44]

Grace is therefore, quite simply, the presence and power of God in our lives, enlightening, judging, forgiving, empowering, sustaining, comforting, perfecting, loving us in ways that transform our very being and thus enlarge the sphere and effectiveness of our actions.

To make his point even more clearly, Wesley specifies a whole new category of occasions through which we can experience the power of God working in our lives. In addition to the "instituted" means of grace—the list that includes the traditional religious activities of participating in the sacraments, Bible reading, prayer, fasting, and religious conversation (even that list is somewhat broadened from the usual)—he opens up new possibilities by listing examples of what he calls "prudential" means of grace. The examples are instructive: using the arts of holy living; attending class or band meetings and meeting with the congregation of believers; and exercising every part of our office in the society. He summarizes these prudential opportunities to experience God's power in a short list: watching against sin; denying ourselves through temperance; taking up our cross daily; and generally "exercising the presence of God." He concludes: "Never can you use these means but a blessing will ensue. And the more you use them, the more will you grow in grace."[45]

We could expand this list of examples of prudential means of grace to include any occasion that is an opportunity to experience or "exercise" the presence of God. To these examples of prudential means of grace, we could add many other ways that people experience the presence and power of God: studying, preaching, teaching, singing, and visiting the sick, the poor, the prisoners, and the elderly.

Wesley explained the importance of visiting the poor as a means of grace very clearly to Miss March in 1776. She was a well-to-do woman whose upper-class prejudices led her to be hesitant about actually visiting the poor, instead of simply sending them food, clothes, or money. She would much rather spend her time in improving her mind, which Wesley generally would not discourage. But he saw an opportunity for her to grow in grace in new ways. He advised Miss March to value improving her knowledge, but that is nothing compared to love. He writes to her rather forcefully:

> Aim at love and you will not stop at the threshold of perfection. There are many blessings in life, but how do you improve them to the glory of God? And are you willing to know? Then I will tell you how. Go and see the poor and such in their own poor little hovels. Take up your cross, woman! Remember the faith! Jesus went before you, and will go with you. Put off the gentlewoman. You bear a higher character.[46]

Wesley points out a crucial reality in the divine-human relationship: in such circumstances, Christ will go with us. Such visiting will be a means of grace to both the prisoner and to one who visits, for Christ will go with you to him or her. The presence/power of God will become known in the experience of both. These prudential means of grace are not essential, not divinely instituted. Rather they are wise and effective means that can open our lives to the presence and power of God in our lives. By not being "instituted," Wesley says, prudential means of grace allow for more flexibility; and the chances are greater that they will not become dead or formal obligations or activities.[47]

As a Holistic Ministry

As is clear from the foregoing discussion, Wesley's view of visiting the prisons was part of his holistic view of ministry. He was concerned with more than just the spiritual needs of the people, or their physical needs or economic or psychological state. He knew that, as a minister of Christ, he was called to minister to *all* the needs of his neighbor. And he also knew that many times the obvious problem had roots or repercussions in other areas.

The Wesleyan ministry to the prisons, therefore, exhibited the breadth of concerns that was typical of the Methodists' work with the people, rich and poor alike. His mission was a vital combination of concern for the spiritual, medical, monetary, social, educational, familial, and physical well-being of the persons who were imprisoned. To the prisoners, as to the sick, the orphans, the aged, and the shut-ins, the Methodists brought books to read, clothes to wear, food to eat, money to help pay debts, the Eucharist to feed their souls, and Bibles to nourish their hearts and minds. The work in the prisons was a rich combination of preaching and counseling, evangelism and administering the sacraments, talking with keepers and families—all in an effort to try to free them from unjust imprisonment and to open their hearts to freedom from sin and guilt.

And just as the prison ministry reflected the broad concerns of the Wesleys' mission to reform the nation (especially the church), so too their theology reflected the imagery that was strongest in the prisons: the imagery of bondage and liberty. Some of the lines in Charles Wesley's most powerful hymns burst with energy from these prison images:

Long my imprisoned spirit lay,
    Fast bound in sin and nature's night.
Thine eye diffused a quick'ning ray;
    I woke; the dungeon flamed with light.
My chains fell off, my heart was free,
I rose, went forth, and followed thee.[48]

And from the hymn that Charles wrote on the first anniversary of his conversion:

He breaks the power of cancelled sin,
    He sets the prisoner free;
His blood can make the foulest clean—
    His blood availed for me.[49]

Conclusion

The early Methodists might be criticized for not being more on the cutting edge in their day in fighting the many injustices built into the eighteenth-century British penal system. But they were in fact on the front edge of the work with prisoners, considering them as neighbors in the best scriptural sense of the word. Their motivations and rationale were strictly in keeping with their perceived design to "reform the nation, especially the Church, and to spread scriptural holiness across the land."[50] And their work in the prisons took on the variety of forms that characterized their work in the whole of British society. One cannot fault them for their utter and holistic concern for the life, present and eternal, of every person in society as an important part of God's creation.

NOTES

1. Harry Potter, *Hanging in Judgment: Religion and the Death Penalty in England from the Bloody Code to Abolition* (London: SCM Press, 1993), 3–4. See the chart in John Howard, *The State of the Prisons in England and Wales* (Warringtron: Eyers, 1777), 482–83.

2. Tim Macquiban, "Imprisonment and Release in the Writings of the Wesleys," in *Retribution, Repentance, and Reconciliation,* ed. Kate Cooper and Jeremy Gregory (Woodbridge: Boydell, 2004), 241.

3. Notice, for instance, that Charles Wesley mentions his preaching "the condemned sermon" at Newgate Prison, Bristol, to twenty criminals who, he felt, all "died penitent." He goes on to say, however, that twenty more will be executed the following week! Letter to John Fletcher, May 1785.

4. Wesley begins the first and last sections of his sermon on "The Great Assize" with a few words praising the judge and officers of the court as "ministers of God to us for good, the grand supporters of the public tranquility, the patrons of innocence and virtue, the great security of all our temporal blessings." John Wesley, Sermon 15, IV.1, in *The Works of John Wesley* (Nashville: Abingdon, 1975–), 1:371; cited hereinafter as *Works.*

5. John Wesley, *Journal and Diaries I,* in *Works,* 18:124. John Wesley soon discovered that his father, Samuel, had also visited the prisons while a student at Exeter College in Oxford, and advised his son, "Go then, in God's name, in the path to which your Saviour has directed you, and that track wherein your father has gone before you!" Ibid., 126.

6. John reported this development to his father in December 1730. See *Letters I,* in *Works,* 25:259.

7. Letter to Richard Morgan, Sr., *Letters I,* in *Works,* 25:335–42.

8. John Gambold, "The Character of Mr. John Wesley," *The Methodist Magazine* 21 (1798):119–20.

9. See Richard P. Heitzenrater, "The Name Methodist," in *Mirror and Memory* (Nashville: Kingswood Books, 1989), ch. 1.

10. See letter of August 1, 1732, *Letters I,* in *Works,* 25:332–33.

11. Letter, John Clayton to John Wesley, Sept. 4, 1732, in Nehemiah Curnock, ed., *Journal of John Wesley* (London: Epworth Press, 1960), 8:279; see also "John Wesley and the Oxford Methodists, 1725–35" (Durham: Ph.D. dissertation, Duke University, 1972), ch. 10, "The Life and Work of the Oxford Methodists."

12. Wesley himself was not opposed to imprisoning people for crimes actually committed. The records from Newgate Prison in London, newly released on the Internet, include three records of charges being brought by John Wesley against people who had stolen goods from him or from his house. He lost all three cases.

13. MS Oxford Diary 4, March 21–29, 1734, in Methodist Archives, Rylands University Library of Manchester.

14. *Journal and Diaries II,* in *Works,* 19:362. Wesley's Journal gives a narrative account of the event: "On Wednesday my brother and I went, at their earnest desire, to do the last good office to the condemned malefactors. It was the most glorious instance I ever saw of faith triumphing over sin and death.

One observing the tears run fast down the cheeks of one of them in particular, while his eyes were steadily fixed upwards, a few moments before he died, asked, 'How do you feel your heart now?' He calmly replied, 'I feel a peace which I could not have believed to be possible. And I know it is the peace of God which passeth all understanding.'" Eleven prisoners were executed that day for murder and other violent crimes. Ibid., 20–21.

15. *Journal and Diaries II*, in *Works*, 19:100.

16. See Wesley's lengthy account of Sarah Peters's work with the prisoners, especially John Lancaster, in *Journal and Diaries III*, November 13, 1748, in *Works*, 20:252–60. For a sketch of the role of other women reformers, see Potter, *Hanging in Judgment*, 26–28.

17. See Silas Told, *An Account of the Life and Dealings of God with Silas Told* (London: Gilbert and Plummer, 1785).

18. Howard, *State of the Prisons in England and Wales*.

19. To the editor of the *Morning Chronicle*, Nov. 4, 1759, in Telford, *Letters*, 4:78.

20. *Journal and Diaries IV*, Oct. 24, 1760, in *Works*, 21:285.

21. Letter of February 18, 1760, in Telford, *Letters*, 4:84.

22. Letter of January 2, 1761, in Telford, *Letters*, 4:127–28.

23. Letter of October 20, 1759, in Telford, *Letters*, 4:73.

24. Wesley, "A Word to a Condemned Malefactor," in *The Works of the Rev. John Wesley*, ed. Thomas Jackson (London: Wesleyan Conference Office, 1872), 11:179, 181–82, cited hereinafter as *Works* (Jackson).

25. Sermon 3, II.3, in *Works*, 1:147. See Macquiban, "Imprisonment and Release in the Writings of the Wesleys," 245–49, for a more extensive discussion of this theme.

26. Wesley, "Nature, Design, and General Rules," *The Methodist Societies*, in *Works*, 11:72. These Rules are still in force in United Methodism, including the expectation "to visit them that are sick or in prison." See *The Book of Discipline of The United Methodist Church—2008* (Nashville: The United Methodist Publishing House, 2008), 72–74.

27. Wesley, Sermon 84, "The Important Question," III.5, in *Works*, 3:191.

28. See Leonard Hulley, *To Be and To Do: Exploring Wesley's Thought on Ethical Behaviour* (Pretoria: University of South Africa, 1988).

29. *Journal and Diaries I*, in *Works*, 18:126.

30. John records reading the lengthy poem in June 1729. The committee had been appointed four months earlier, and had a painting of its gathering painted by William Hogarth. The poem was published in Samuel Wesley, Jr., *Poems on Several Occasions* (London: 1736), 173–91.

31. Ibid., 188.

32. John Wesley, *Explanatory Notes upon the New Testament* (London: W. Bowyer, 1755), note at Matt. 25:30.

33. Strangely, when Wesley preaches his sermon on "The Great Assize" before the court sessions in Bedford in 1758, he quotes this passage describing the final judgment day but omits the last two items, visiting the sick and those in prison. Sermon 15, II.8, in *Works*, 1:368.

34. Wesley, *Explanatory Notes*, on Heb. 13:3.

35. Wesley, *Explanatory Notes*, on Luke 10:37.

36. Wesley, Sermon 92, "On Zeal," III.9., in *Works*, 3:319.

37. Wesley, Sermon 98, "On Visiting the Sick," III.4–5, in *Works*, 3:394.

38. Ibid., I–I.3, in *Works*, 3:387.

39. Ibid., I.3–4, 388.

40. Ibid., I–I.3, 387.

41. Wesley, Sermon 25, "Upon our Lord's Sermon on the Mount, 5," II.3, in *Works*, 1:554–55.

42. Wesley, Sermon 98, "On Visiting the Sick," ¶1, in *Works*, 3:385.

43. He is explaining the text, 2 Cor. 1:12, "By the grace of God, we have had our conversation in the world."

44. Sermon 12, "The Witness of Our Own Spirit," ¶15, in *Works*, 1:309.

45. Wesley, "Minutes of Several Conversations," Qu. 48 and Answer, in *Works* (Jackson), 8:323.

46. See Wesley's letter to Miss March, June 9, 1775, in Telford, *Letters*, 6:153.

47. Wesley, *A Plain Account of the People Called Methodists*, II.9, in *Works*, 8:262–63.

48. "And Can it Be," verse 4, in *A Collection of Hymns for the People Called Methodists*, in *Works*, 7:323.

49. "O for a Thousand Tongues to Sing," verse 4, in *Collection*, in *Works*, 7:80.

50. Wesley, "Minutes of Several Conversations," Qu. 3 and Answer, in *Works* (Jackson), 8:299.

CHAPTER 6

Prison Ministry In The United Methodist Church: Perceptions, Provocations, and Prognostications

PATRICIA BARRETT

went to jail for the first time in 1970. I had called campus security about an intruder and felt some responsibility for his incarceration. So I took the bus to the county jail to see what I could do to help. The intruder had long since been released, but the warden seemed eager to show me around. Most inmates, he told me, seldom had visitors; and he suggested that I consider visiting regularly. The invitation caught my interest; and, with a fellow seminarian, I started going to jail. Thus began my long relationship with prison ministry and criminal justice work.

In what follows, I write neither as an expert in the field of prison ministry nor as a scholar in criminal justice, nor even as a professional chaplain. Rather, I write as a practitioner who has experienced and provided leadership in the areas of prison ministry and criminal justice for over thirty-seven years on a variety of levels inside and outside the church—from working face-to-face with prisoners to representing chaplains in New Jersey state institutions to serving as the endorsing agent for The United Methodist Church. As my responsibilities have changed, so has my vantage point. In the next few pages, I recount this multifaceted narrative, combining experience, reflection, commentary, and prognostication to offer insights that I trust will serve the next generation of United Methodist experts, scholars, and practitioners in our church's ongoing commitment to prison and criminal justice ministries.

Going to Jail

Morris County in the 1970s was home to several colleges and universities. Located close enough to New York City for commuting and far away enough for comfort, the county was fairly quiet. Morris County Jail was small, with a daily population of about one hundred (mostly male) prisoners, the majority awaiting some court action. In those days, public drunkenness could land one in jail; and we had a number of "winter regulars" for whom the jail had become a second home of sorts. The law changed a few years later, turning a lot of these regulars out on the streets. I began to wonder how these ex-prisoners were faring on the streets. The country had just moved into a time when the rights of the mentally ill were becoming an issue of public concern. Morris County Jail was near a large psychiatric hospital. We were coming to the end of the era of such massive institutions, which were sometimes condemned as "snake pits." The community seemed ready to explore alternative ways of dealing with the marginalized.

The energies of the anti-war and civil rights movements resulted in a growing interest in citizen action in many arenas, including corrections. Morris County Jail did not have a chaplain on staff; but the local clergy association funded a seminarian to visit the jail and provide worship services and counseling. While I was working in the jail, the sponsoring churches expressed an interest in volunteering, and soon we had teaching, counseling, work release, and post-release programs. Several area congregations and the regional office of Bell Labs provided so many volunteers that at one point we had more than two volunteers on the roll for every inmate. The local newspaper ran feature articles on programs in the jail on a regular basis.

The jail staff generally supported the volunteer effort. At the same time, plans were drawn up to provide professional training for correction officers. Even the language was changing: We no longer spoke of "guards" but of "correction officers." At the same time, prisons were not in any sense popular and employees were not held in high regard in the community. Often they were viewed as inferior to law enforcement officers and only slightly better than the inmates. In those times, there was little enthusiasm in the community for prisons or halfway houses or treatment centers. NIMBY ("not in my backyard") was the going mantra.

Inside the jail there was a sense of possibility. With so many "visitors," the warden decided to fix up the jail, painting walls with bright colors and even creating a mural to welcome visitors. Somehow these improvements brought the jail to the attention of New York's Parsons School of Design, and I was invited to spend time with the students as they were designing the new wing for women at the Rikers Island facility. Their research determined that components such as space, light, and color have a significant impact on how prisoners cope while incarcerated. They even determined that single-cell arrangements work best for men and that dormitory conditions were most effective for women.

At the time, I was continuing my seminary studies and had requested that my work with the jail be considered my field placement. My request was turned down. This work, I was told, did not qualify as a supervised ministry experience, since there was no one to supervise me. I was blessed, however, to have had two faculty members—Dr. Dave Graybeal and Dr. Tom Oden—who volunteered to work with me; and together we reviewed my daily journal for a year. It was an education for all of us.

Putting in Time with the State

I was invited to work with the Commissioner of the Department of Institutions and Agencies of the State of New Jersey. Her responsibilities included all the state residential institutions (correctional, mental health, mental retardation, and veterans services). My job was to oversee chaplaincy and religious services in all those institutions. At that time mental-health chaplains were expected to have completed clinical training. There were no corresponding expectations for prison chaplains. I even discovered paperwork indicating that prison chaplains were more likely to be selected for their political party loyalty than for their expertise or training. There were no hiring standards for chaplains and no standards for religious practice in the prisons.

Yet times were a-changing, and it was not long before I had my first taste of First Amendment issues in prison ministry. The First Amendment to the Constitution of the United States is a double-edged sword. On the one hand, it calls for clear separation of church and state by prohibiting the establishment of a state religion. On the other hand, the courts have consistently ruled that citizens have the freedom to practice the religion of their choice.

The 1970s saw the waning of the reasonably comfortable religious demarcation of Protestant–Catholic–Jew that had shaped American culture. I have long believed that prisons are the canaries in the coal mine of our culture and the changes during the 1970s proved predictors of our current dilemmas. The chaplains, the state council of churches, staff from the personnel section of the Department, and I worked together to develop two critical documents: one outlined new professional standards (and salary scales) and hiring practices for chaplains and the other set standards for religious practices in the prisons. The growing Muslim inmate population required that we develop new relationships within the Muslim community outside the prison and rework our hiring standards and our standards of practice.

This era also brought the parachurch organization into prominence, most conspicuously with Charles Colson's Prison Fellowship. The number of religious volunteers grew as parachurch organizations drew volunteers from congregations without prior experience in such ministry. A distance began to set in between the chaplain—responsible for the religious practice of all the inmates—and the community volunteer, who represented a particular theological perspective and "audience."

Community involvement in prisons and post-release programs seemed to peak during these years, bolstered by grants available from the Law Enforcement Assistance Administration. Many prisons employed volunteer coordinators to manage the burgeoning number of programs, although the largest group of volunteers continued to be in the "religious" category. But by the end of the decade the money was drying up and public patience was eroding as well. Some prisons discontinued volunteer coordinator positions and expected chaplains to serve in that capacity, since the large majority of volunteers were "religious." Long-term change requires long-term commitment; and being "soft on crime" was becoming a favorite insult in the political arena, especially as the economy turned sour.

While working for the state, I had my first experience with the establishment of a denominational congregation inside an institution. One of our chaplains announced that his denomination had formally established a congregation in his institution. This raised a number of concerns about his role. As an employed chaplain he was responsible to serve all of the prisoners, regardless of faith tradition. Yet as a denominational pastor he had responsibilities to his denomination's congregation in the facility. The issue remained a muddle when I moved on to another position; but it opened up a new set of considerations when I considered how best to build bridges between the prisoner population on the inside and "free world" community congregations.

During my tenure with the state, New Jersey became committed to the concept of "de-institutionalization" in the mental-health field. The rule of thumb was that persons would be committed to a state psychiatric hospital only if they were "a danger to themselves or others." The intention was to diminish the role of the large hospital and to develop community-based resources such as community mental-health centers, small-group homes, and transitional facilities. The advent of new psychotropic medications seemed to offer the possibility of more humane ways of treating the mentally ill. Ultimately, the balance failed. While institutions were downsized or closed, the community services lagged behind. The result was a growing number of mentally ill persons moving into the jails and prisons.

While working for the state, I was a probationary member of my annual conference, having been ordained a deacon in 1970. In order to receive ordination as an elder and full membership in the annual conference I needed to serve under supervision for two years. But who knew enough about what I was doing to supervise me? After talking with Bishop Dale White and my district superintendent Dr. Clark Hunt, we created a supervising team that included a member of the conference who was serving in a similar position in another state. (I believe I got more supervision than my colleagues in the ordination track!)

The View From the General Church

In 1980 I joined the staff of the Division of Chaplains and Related Ministries at the United Methodist General Board of Higher Education and Ministry, in Nashville, Tennessee. I joked that I was moving into "deep church" when I shifted from state government to a denominational agency. While in seminary, I had written my polity paper on how the church had failed to address relationships with persons in specialized settings, such as chaplaincy. I believed that being in this new position would provide me with an opportunity to make a difference.

For fifteen years my focus had been on working with chaplains and pastoral counselors in many settings, including prisons and jails. It is trite but true that we frequently perceive reality from our location, assuming that everywhere is just like where we are. Moving from a small state to a national entity was an education. For one thing, as I started to relate to state and county institutions all over the country, I saw my own experience in prison chaplaincy borne out. I also had my first contact with the Federal Bureau of Prisons, considered at that time the "Cadillac of Corrections." There I saw not only high standards for hiring and practice but also programs of continuing education and systems of support that made state and county chaplains green with envy. While local community programs seemed to be declining, the Bureau still had volunteer coordinators, clinically trained chaplains, training programs, and standards assuring a key role for religious activities.

My new role provided opportunities to visit chaplains in their institutions and at meetings of the American Correctional Chaplains Association (the professional association affiliated with the American Correctional Association). I soon realized that the prison chaplains had several concerns and needs in common. Most felt isolated, the majority serving as sole chaplain in their institutions with little support from local clergy. Certainly the state and county chaplains were receiving lower salaries than chaplains in other settings and much less support for continuing education and professional relationships. The majority felt alienated from the annual conference. Mainline denominations, including The United Methodist Church, were disappearing from prison ministry. It has been said that people working in law enforcement and corrections absorb some of the stigma attached to felons and prisoners. Chaplains are not immune from that stigma, either.

Working at the general church level opened up a global dimension; and I visited prisons in central conferences such as Liberia, Germany, the Philippines, and Russia. I was active in the creation of the International Prison Chaplains Association (IPCA). The initial IPCA gathering brought together chaplains from fifty-one countries on five continents and from a variety of Christian communions. During a community-building session with a group of about twenty-five chaplains, I heard a familiar complaint: "My fellow pastors say I have left the ministry." Chaplains from Africa, Europe, the Middle East, New Zealand, and North America immediately agreed, claiming their common pain and anger. Although holding varying standards, practices, and theological assumptions, they shared a sense of isolation from the churches that sent them forth.

While visiting prisons in other countries, I marveled at the way prisons express culture. In Liberia, a country with a long relationship with the United States, the prisons at first looked familiar, with a perimeter security design that would have fit right in with early American prisons, for example the classic Philadelphia model, with guard towers, gates, and armed tower guards. Upon entering the facility, however, I discovered an open-air environment, more like a Liberian village than the cell houses with which I was familiar. The

same was true in the Philippines, where the structure of the institution was shaped as much by the climate as by the standards of security. In both cases there was much more access for families than in
the standard U.S. prison. In Russia I found a more familiar model,
but with more regimentation and uniformity. Where the United
States relies more on single-cell systems in high-security institutions,
the Russian prisons tended to house inmates in dormitory style and
gather them in large groups. Our worship services drew much larger
congregations than would ever have attended worship in an
American prison.

The General Board of Higher Education and Ministry sponsored
a consultation on prison ministry in the post-Communist context,
which drew United Methodist pastors and prison volunteers from
ten Eastern European countries. The event, held at Prison #2 in
Ekaterinburg, Russia, was especially meaningful as I was blessed to
watch, listen, and learn how Christians—some new to the faith,
many new to ministry, all creating new relationships with public
institutions in a time of new beginnings—bring to birth a ministry of
"visiting those in prison." The warden of Prison #2 provided a
keynote address, in which he noted that the role of the prison is not
to punish (that would be redundant) but to transform and prepare
persons to return to society. What I longed to hear once again in the
U.S., I was hearing in central Russia!

Serving as Endorsing Agent

In 1997 I became the Endorsing Agent for The United Methodist
Church, heading up the United Methodist Endorsing Agency, which
is part of the General Board of Higher Education and Ministry. In
this position I engaged more with standards and systems and somewhat less directly with chaplains in their settings. A significant
portion of my time is in consultation with endorsers from other faith
communities, building shared language and values on ministries
of pastoral care in specialized settings, including prisons. My office
has hosted a few consultations, bringing prison chaplains together
for sharing, learning, and support. These experiences showed that

chaplains in corrections continue to struggle with issues in that setting: ever-expanding numbers of religious groups needing resourcing; reduced staff and increased workload; reduction in the perceived value of chaplain ministry; limited opportunities for continuing professional education; and the sense of disconnection from the clergy covenant community.

The years since 1970 witnessed a growth in prisons. In the two decades after I left New Jersey, the number of state institutions tripled. The national rate of incarceration exploded (the United States now leads the world in per-capita incarceration rates), sentences lengthened, the death penalty returned with a vengeance (the United States remains one of the dwindling number of nations practicing execution), and the "military-industrial complex" of the Vietnam era was transformed into today's "prison-industrial complex."

Economics had become entwined with the prison system. Consequently, communities that once fought prison construction in their neighborhoods now compete for the jobs new prisons introduce into local economies. We have also seen the inception of the "private" prison, once inconceivable, now traded on the stock market. Although expected to conform to professional ACA (American Correctional Association) standards, few employ professional chaplains and some utilize community clergy, paying them hourly at minimum wage.

Perceptions, Provocations, and Prognostications

I close with a set of perceptions, provocations, and prognostications on the future of prison ministry in The United Methodist Church. I offer these reflections in hopes that they will contribute to a renewal of United Methodism's historic commitment to prison ministry and criminal justice work.

The Connection

Chaplaincy differs from pastoral ministry in a local church in several ways. The mission of the church is to "make disciples of Jesus Christ for the transformation of the world."[1] Chaplains work in institutions and systems whose missions differ from that of the church. Pastors serve in congregations of people who have *chosen* to participate in that faith community. By contrast, the mission of the prison is to isolate individuals from the community in an institution where they live out their sentences, forfeiting their freedom. Chaplains serve all the people in the institution, regardless of their faith community. Chaplains minister to those who do not get to pick their pastors. Some labor in settings where the mission may be far from the mission of the church. Fundamentally, chaplains serve God and God's people, representing the church and the sacred in secular settings.

The ministry of the church to the incarcerated and the witness of the church to the criminal justice system call for several ways of being involved, from the volunteer visitors from a congregation to the ordained clergyperson serving as an institutional chaplain to the social-action activists shining an often-uncomfortable light on the injustices of the justice system. In my experience, it has often been the case that these three expressions of the church's presence and witness have seldom been able to join together in holistic action. In a connectional church, we ought to be able to do better.

Where do we go from here? Jesus' words recorded in the Gospel of Matthew make it clear that we are to visit those in prison because in doing so we serve Jesus there. Let us lay aside our differences to respond to Jesus' command. But we need to do more. We need to transform our differences into a collaborative effort. As Paul reminds us, we are one body with many parts (1 Cor. 12:12-31). None of the parts is the whole body; and the body is complete only when the parts work together. Therefore, we need to bring together the congregations, the chaplains, the social activists, and the seminaries (our centers for theological and biblical reflection) to develop a unified response to the incarcerated and the systems that establish and maintain incarceration. Our failure to do this will result in our failure to respond in a holistic way to Jesus' expectation. Such collaboration includes critical attention to each component, as well as serious mutual support in a spirit of humility. The aim of the book you're reading is to argue for just such a holistic approach.[2]

The Congregation and the Prison

I have seen several models of relationship between congregation and prison over the years. Individual congregations have sponsored volunteer programs inside the institution and for persons being released. In some instances, a local council of churches provides financial support for chaplaincy, especially where jails do not have a staff chaplain. In some cases, these chaplains function in a classic way as staff chaplains, while, in other cases, they are seen by the institution as volunteer visiting clergy.

Currently, there is a movement to establish denominational congregations inside institutions. One Presbyterian church has established a congregation located adjacent to a prison, providing ministries inside and to families who come to visit their incarcerated loved ones. A United Methodist example is the "Women at the Well" congregation, established by the Iowa annual conference in the state women's prison. There the pastor is not the institutional chaplain but an elder appointed to the charge. Several congregations in the annual conference provide financial support. While this effort may not fit the usual "church-growth" criteria, it is certainly a missional initiative.

John Wesley's movement was characterized by the communities of support and accountability (classes and bands) he developed. It seems to me that, through this means, he made disciples who then became engaged in works of mercy and justice. Can The United Methodist Church choose to establish new congregations within prisons and among the families of prisoners? This would surely be a powerful marriage of mission and church growth! What would it mean for an annual conference to establish congregations inside prisons or adjacent to them?

A few annual conferences have significant programs that coordinate congregational involvement in jails and prisons. In several cases Disciple Bible Study programs have been used. What if every annual conference expanded its current programs of Disciple to include prisoners or their families?

Such initiatives should be supported and celebrated denominationwide. While some effort has been made to collect information about what is being done within The United Methodist Church relative to prison ministry, the undertaking needs sustained attention and support.

The Basics

We require a three-pronged commitment of endorsed chaplains and pastoral counselors: continuing spiritual formation, intellectual formation, and professional formation. This is essential for everyone engaged in ministries within the criminal justice system, whether as volunteers or as professionals, whether inside the institution or in the community. The United Methodist Church must provide the resources for sustaining this continuing formation through the efforts of our theological and spiritual leaders. Engaging the criminal justice system at any point is a significant challenge. Here we encounter the brokenness of culture, community, and individuals. All cry out for justice; all seek mercy, and few receive either.

The complexity and ambiguity of the issues can be deeply discouraging. Our culture places a high value on efficiency and results. Prison treatment programs are evaluated on their impact on recidivism, often over a short period of time. The transformation of a human life and the birthing of community do not produce immediate results (some apparent success does not stand the test of time). Sustained presence in prisons will be marked by seasons of "failure." We cannot expect to be propelled by success as defined by culture. From the beginning our movement into prison must be a faith response, undergirded with perpetual prayer and reflection. Our service will probably not produce the immediate fruit we so deeply desire. Yet, despite our longing for success, our primary calling is to faithfulness.

The United Methodist Church needs a center to collect and develop spiritual-formation resources for persons working within the criminal justice system; to train and support volunteers and congregations; to prepare and sustain persons engaged in chaplain ministry; to bring together those who serve with prisoners, victims, and law enforcement; and to find a way to bring together within the rubric of faith and practice those who serve in disparate places. What would it mean for our theological education if faculty, administrators, and students routinely addressed questions of justice in both theoretical and practical ways? What would it mean if bishops and cabinets expected clergy to respond in the affirmative when asked if they visit those in prison? How can we reclaim the fervor of the Wesleys by returning to prison and discovering our roots?

Is There Hope?

Is there hope for chaplains? For many years, I have been involved in the task of raising standards, expectations, and training for chaplains. Recently I have watched as those standards, expectations, and training have diminished and, in some cases, have disappeared. Not too long ago I learned that one state considered a GED a sufficient educational requirement for employment as an institutional chaplain. I have seen state governments move from employing chaplains to utilizing contracts for community clergy, or to converting the job description of chaplain to that of religious coordinator. I have watched the virtual disappearance of clinical pastoral education (CPE) in correctional facilities. I have observed the continuing struggle of the American Correctional Chaplains Association (ACCA) to maintain a high level of professional competence and education. I have witnessed the number of endorsed United Methodist prison chaplains cut in half through attrition so that currently there are no endorsed United Methodist chaplains in the juvenile justice system in the United States. My hope is that The United Methodist Church will choose to embrace this ministry by identifying, preparing, supporting, and affirming persons for appointment to prison chaplaincy. This must include salary support considerations, as prison chaplain salaries are generally significantly lower when compared to other chaplain salaries.

Is there hope for prisons? I have seen the enthusiasm of the 1970s, with its energy for rehabilitation and transformation, collapse into the choice for quarantine and isolation from the "free world." It seems to me that our society has always isolated the "different," creating institutions to contain them and protect the rest of us. As people of faith and disciples of Jesus Christ we are called to define community in a different way. Until we incarnate that belief through our living and service these divisions will continue to inhibit the kingdom of God. Restoration and transformation require our active presence across the dividing walls, including the walls of the prison.

Is there hope for the church? When I began my ministry, I worked within a community of several faiths. Although our doctrines and polity differed, we always found common ground for ministering together because our primary concern was service. Over the years that faith community has expanded both within and beyond the Judeo-Christian rubric. With that expansion has come competition and partisanship. Years ago, a chaplain with many years of service, spoke about the diversity among his religious volunteers: "Who they are is so loud I cannot hear what they are saying." He said this because, although they had different doctrines, they shared a common compassion and commitment to the prisoners and respect for one another. Admittedly, there have always been individuals in small groups who criticized other small groups; but until recently they were in the minority. Nowadays, differences seem to focus more on the "rights" of chaplains than on the care of the people we are called to serve. I find this development deeply discouraging. Traditionally, the mainline denominations have led in bringing together the diversity of faith communities. Yet the number of chaplains and congregations from the mainline denominations serving in criminal justice ministry has diminished. The United Methodist Church must reclaim its presence in this ministry and provide leadership to a fresh commitment to ministries of justice and mercy.

Is there hope? When I first entered the world of corrections, I was warned against being a naïve bleeding heart, advised to assume that everything I heard was designed to mislead me, and reminded that the inmates were criminal offenders. During my first year working in the jail, I kept a journal, being careful not to read what I had written until the year had come to an end. I wanted to see if my attitudes and assumptions had changed. To my horror, they had. That was an enduring lesson for me. The second lesson came when I led a brief devotional on the parable of the sower. At the time, we had a program designed to teach decision-making skills. The first phase was an intensive weekend marathon, where volunteers spent two days in the jail. At the end of the last session, we had a debriefing time, closing with a devotional. Everything had gone well; the volunteers were enthusiastic, each seeing signs of growth and change in the prisoners. As I read the text—"A sower went out to sow" (Mark 4:3)—I was struck by the part that notes that some seeds spring up fast but wither in the heat, while others, after a time, do sprout, grow, and bear fruit. The text was reminding us that we are called to be faithful, rather than to seek for signs that we have been successful. From time to time, that wisdom returns to me, especially on the occasions when I begin to take credit for myself.

Is there hope? Certainly! We are called to visit Jesus in prison. Our presence makes a difference, as does our absence. Although certainly laudable, the intent to reduce recidivism and criminal behavior and to transform the criminal justice system and the lives of those wrapped up in it is not enough for those who seek to follow God's call to be with those in prison. The presence and witness of the people of God in such places is a reminder that the creation God loves is not divided by walls and bars. And living out the Kingdom is planting seeds that will—surely they will—produce fruit.

We have the structures. We have the resources. We have the call. There is hope if we respond, taking the open doors, open hearts, and open minds to the places of locked doors, where minds are made up and hearts wait to be opened.

NOTES

1. *The Book of Discipline of The United Methodist Church—2008* (Nashville: The United Methodist Publishing House, 2008), ¶120.

2. Part of the fracturing of our ministry, says Russell Richey in a recent book, has to do with the increasing marginalization of extension ministers (including chaplains) in the overall work of the annual conference and the church as a whole. Reintegrating these diverse ministries "beyond the local church" into the

connectional ministry covenant is essential in recovering a holistic vision of ministry for our day. See Russell E. Richey, *Extension Ministers: Mr. Wesley's True Heirs* (Nashville: The General Board of Higher Education and Ministry, The United Methodist Church, 2008).

Section 4

Ministry
Perspectives

CHAPTER 7

To See and To Be Seen

JANET WOLF

W hat does it mean to see prisons, prison officials, and those who are incarcerated through a pastoral-care lens? What does pastoral care with those inside prisons look like in a country that incarcerates a higher percentage of black men than South Africa did under apartheid? As James Lawson[1] often remarks, both Jesus and Martin Luther King, Jr., engaged systems and structures and narrow theologies and powers of death *because* of their pastoral connections—because they knew intimately the hurt and pain, the struggles and sorrows, the deep despair and ongoing hope of the people. Their pastoral care led them to listen to, learn from, and identify with those who were pushed to the edges of life and, as a consequence of those relationships, confront powers and principalities.

It is not easy. So many myths and stereotypes get in the way. High and solid walls have been built by racism, classism, and "prisonization." Prisons intentionally separate, segregate, and disconnect the imprisoned from families and communities. And in spite of the clear command from Jesus to come to and visit with those in prison, the church keeps its distance. Less than 20 percent of those incarcerated ever have a visitor from the outside.

This chapter is a collection of voices and stories from inside the prison system. While names have been changed, the people chose to share their stories with you and served as initial editors for this chapter. They hope that their stories will shatter stereotypes, dismantle myths, alter worldviews, and challenge people to reevaluate what they think they know about who is behind prison walls and what happens inside. Most of all, they hope that people will take action to change the system.

Three different contexts have provided the stories and voices included:

- interviews with correctional officers, high-level administrators, and individual inmates;
- graduate theology classes held in the state's maximum security prison (Riverbend Maximum Security Institution, with approximately 12 students from the inside and 12 students from Vanderbilt Divinity School and the community; these classes were started in January 2003 and have been offered every semester [fall, spring, summer] since then);[2]
- undergraduate criminal justice classes held in the state's minimum security prerelease prison (Charles Bass Correctional Complex Annex, with about 22 students from the inside and 22 from American Baptist College and the community; these classes started in January 2005 and continue each fall and spring semester.)[3]

The model used in both classes is the same:

- A community is created that is deliberately relational, requiring mutuality.
- Those who are incarcerated are primary partners in decisions and leadership.
- Professors are animators and co-facilitators.
- Pedagogy is participatory and communal.

- All participants commit to a partnership *with* people, in contrast to any version of ministry *to* or *for* people.
- Participants enter into an intentional covenant that creates a safe space; welcomes all voices; practices confidentiality; and honors each person, specifically noting that everyone is a teacher and everyone a learner.
- One explicit outcome is the development of a theological and sociological critique of the criminal justice system from the inside.
- Classes focus on transformative justice.[4]

Learning to See

In South Africa, a common Zulu greeting is "*sawabona.*" And the response is "*sikona.*" *Sawabona* means "I see you." *Sikona* means "I am here." In a world where those inside prisons and jails are most often invisible, what might it mean for those of us on the outside to see— *really* see—the faces, stories, scars and dreams, hurts and hopes of those who are locked up? To come close enough, to listen long enough, to be able to declare: "I see you!" And to invite those inside to respond: "I am here, fully present, being me—not a number, not identified by my charge or my sentence, not an object for your charity or proselytizing, but a human being, willing to be seen, being me, really me." What might it mean to *see* the more than 2 million human beings locked away behind razor wire and prison walls?

Closing the distance, beginning to see, started for me on Christmas Eve 1976. Edgehill United Methodist Church, a small, intentionally interracial, reconciling, urban church I had joined, held Christmas Eve service at the old state prison, "the walls." The pastor, Bill, urged us to attend, emphasizing that the story of the Incarnation, the Word becoming flesh among us—this baby born to an unwed teenage mother among an oppressed, colonized, impoverished people—required a different setting than the inside of our church building. "It belongs in the streets," he said—the body of Christ in, for, and with the world.

Arriving at the prison that night, we were told that we couldn't go inside. Something had happened, and we would have to hold our service outside. And even though this was Nashville, Tennessee, it was snowing. We were a sad, little handful of people, huddled outside the immense prison, snow and sleet swirling around us. This was not my idea of Christmas Eve. For me, Christmas Eve had included brilliant poinsettias and candles lighting up the rafters in the sanctuary. Christmas Eve was trumpets and pageantry, majestic music and bright colors, the choir spilling down the aisle, little kids dressed up like angels and shepherds.

We huddled together, trying to get the Christ-candle lit. The fierce wind extinguished the match every time. Pastor Bill was trying to help shield the flame and handed me the Bible, saying: "Read this." And I did, from Isa. 9:2: "The people who walked in darkness have seen great light; . . . on them light has shined." Just about that time, the Christ-candle took flame; and I leaned in, trying to help my kids light their small candles. But in my heart, I was grumbling, still sure that this moment could not possibly matter to anyone. Then one of my boys tugged on my coat. "Mama, look!" I turned to look where he was pointing and saw, in cell after cell, the glow of matches and lighters being held up to the windows, spilling through the bars. As we began singing "Silent Night, Holy Night," I imagined that I heard voices, inside and out, singing with the joy and awe of those who have turned to see what God is doing in the world.

Breaking through the Barriers

In Matt. 25:44, those who are confronted by the king cry out: "Lord, when was it that we saw you . . . ?" Most of us do not see because we are not present inside the prisons and jails; we are not in relationship with those who are thirsty and hungry, impoverished and marginalized. As Pamela Couture argues, referring to John Wesley, we "keep out of the way of knowing." We distance ourselves, focusing our efforts on charity, which makes us feel good about ourselves while masking our cooperation with the very systems that perpetuate poverty and injustice.[5] Presence is a beginning—but only a beginning. Unless we allow the proximity to be translated into partnership, in ways that challenge and unmask our assumptions, biases, stereotypes and misconceptions, we will not be able to see people on the inside.

For those of us on the outside, barriers include our physical separation from people who are incarcerated, our distance from the prisons and jails, our fear of those who are behind bars, and our assumptions about who is incarcerated and why. Barriers are also offered by the criminal justice system itself, which is preoccupied with security and does not make it easy to actually get inside a prison. The barriers can be intimidating.

It might have been the beginning of any seminary/college class, except that we had passed through five checkpoints inside Riverbend to get here. We were required to show photo identification at the front desk, removing shoes and jackets and laying them, along with books and pens, on the conveyer belt for the screening machine. As we passed through the metal detector, our left hands were stamped with a mark that could only be seen under a special light. One by one we were called into small rooms to be searched and patted down by correctional officers. Then into the metal "cage," a space surrounded by wire, with a gate closing firmly behind the group. And then, after what sometimes seemed a very long moment, the gate in front of us opened and we moved toward the next door. We lifted our hands under a light so that the correctional officers behind a darkened window would unlock the next door. We walked down a long hall, past another checkpoint, waiting for the "click" that meant the next door had been unlocked. Now in the open space between buildings, we walked across the "yard," past the "high side," which houses death row, and on to the "low side." The correctional officers wanted us to keep going—no stopping, no waving, moving past lines of men in blue. We passed the mental-health lockdown ward and then the chapel, a handful of folks listening to vehement preaching. A correctional officer was waiting at the entrance to the building where the class was to be held and he escorted us, unlocking the classroom door. Insiders, scattered along the sidewalk and in the hallway, greeted us with huge grins and outstretched hands of welcome.

For almost six years, longtime prison advocate and restorative justice author Harmon Wray, Lipscomb University history professor Richard Goode, and I have been inviting students from seminaries, colleges, congregations, and the community to come with us inside prisons to learn with and from those who are incarcerated. It started with Harmon Wray's course on "The Theology and Politics of Crime and Justice in America." While Harmon had taught the course for a number of years at Vanderbilt Divinity School, it was not until January 2003 that he moved the course into Riverbend Maximum Security Institution, the state prison that houses death row. Ever since then, students from Vanderbilt Divinity School and the community have been coming to the prison to join students from Riverbend.

We had studied the Sing Sing model developed by New York Theological Seminary—theological education happening inside prison walls[6]—but wanted to add another component, namely, to bring students with us from the outside as partners in learning, in doing theology from the inside out. To prepare and plan for the course, we met with potential Riverbend students for several months before the first class began. It was important, before we started classes, to incorporate insiders as leaders with power to set priorities and boundaries.

From the beginning, the classes startled us. We had not predicted the raw honesty, prophetic truth telling, wide mercy, and healing power that were let loose. We were surprised how quickly strangers, with so many reasons to remain divided, became community. We often noted that the class had become church for us, and we saw that happen for so many others as well. We could not argue that this holy time was something we were orchestrating, although we thought we had some clues about what called such a community into being. Mutuality is the key—believing that everyone brings a gift. Each semester we design a class covenant that reminds us that we are all learners and all teachers; that every single voice is welcomed and valued. This is ministry *with*—not *to* or *for*—the incarcerated. It is an authentic partnership shaped by our desire for justice, not charity, and by our certainty that some of the most profound, prophetic, world-transforming theology is happening behind prison walls.

In the course of many classes, we heard some of the same things over and over. From insiders: "This class is the only place I feel really human." "I never knew who I was until I came to this class. I had so much anger in me, but these classes allowed me to see a side of myself I never even knew existed." "We are always human beings in this class." "I never knew people outside cared." "I never thought I would really matter to anyone." "The classes give us all permission to shine, to believe we've been born to shine."

From outsiders: "I never knew. I thought everyone inside prison was so different from me . . . but it's not true." "I was scared to death to walk in here and then that first day I met people who became family." "This course has changed my life. I will never be the same." "I have been a pastor for more than twenty years, but I never understood what prison ministry really means until now."

The experience of working with correctional administrators and prison officials varies widely. The correctional system is designed to keep people separated, and it is not easy to connect with folks on the inside. It is even more difficult to create safe space for a community of mutuality in an environment of "them or us," an institution in which officers identify themselves as "custodians of prison policy" with largely unchecked power to harass and coerce prisoners. Their job requires a focus on security; and it is all too easy to become rigid in applying the policies. As one correctional officer put it: "I'm disturbed by this whole system. Been working inside for more than twenty years. This place is a warehouse. Reminds me of rounding up cattle off a ranch and putting them in pens. Total chaos. People scared; no one answering questions; no rhyme or reason to lots of stuff here. Lots of correctional officers, even at the top, have a deaf ear—they don't see and don't care. Just wanting to make sure no one escapes. I tell them, you smack a dog on a leash so long; and when he gets off, he's gonna bite you."

The security business tends to attract people who want to enforce the law, who want to have the authority to keep order and be able to require others to follow rules. The work inside a prison is not easy and the pay is not much. It is not uncommon for correctional officers to have to work a double shift with little or no notice.

There is a high turnover among staff and ongoing tension. While there are correctional officers who do care and try their best to work effectively and compassionately, they often seem to be in the minority. It hurts to allow oneself to experience the hardness of the prison. As one correctional officer commented:

> I try to ease pain and give a little hope. I know these guys, and I know it's never too late. I'm no miracle worker but I can listen, care, look deeper into situations and try to get some answers. . . . It's a heartbreaking moment to see children and daddies during visitation. When it's time to leave, everyone's crying. You could slip on all the tears on that floor.

Nevertheless, the system tends to attract people who disconnect from the inside population. Some seem to be quick to exercise their power over and against those on the inside. Oftentimes the exercise of power seems arbitrary, capricious, and unnecessarily harsh. We have seen this pressure intensify as people get closer to their release time. We have struggled to build relationships with correctional officers, chaplains, wardens, and high-level administrators—to work for reconciliation even while confronting people in power in order to break through the barriers.

Orientation is provided for both inside and outside students before classes begin. It is the only time that the students meet separately. The orientation is designed to make sure that people understand the rules and regulations of the prison and the program. It is also an opportunity to express concerns, ask questions, and discuss both fears and hopes. The prison chaplain sometimes asks to participate in the orientation session for outsiders. This has not always been helpful. The following example helps explain why.

In one orientation session, after introductions, during which several people explained their longing to learn from and listen to people who are incarcerated, the particular chaplain began.

> You need to be concerned about everyone in the prison. It's not just prisoners who are incarcerated. You have staff and officers who are incarcerated, locked up with those inmates, under the

influence of criminal felons for eight hours at a time. . . . We do IQ tests, and you're going to be dealing with some people with an IQ of 75.

After going over dress codes and basic rules in the institution, the chaplain added:

You can be charged with a crime if you violate the rules and policies, so you be very careful. . . . Sometimes I wonder if I shouldn't quit my job and go on one of these work-release jobs. Some of these prisoners make more than I do. I know my clerk makes 50 cents an hour; but when I look at some of the accounts for prerelease inmates, I think I should ask for a loan.[7]

And then the chaplain finished:

I believe in rehabilitation but it takes more to change minds. I tell prisoners there's just a 4 to 6 inch difference between you and me: that space between your ears—the choices you've made. I'm sure I can safely say this as a Baptist preacher in a Baptist school, it takes Jesus, getting down on your knees and accepting Jesus as your personal Lord and Savior. That is the only answer.

It was quiet in the room of Christians, Jews, Buddhists, and Muslims. Those who had never been inside a prison and those who had served time and would be going back in for the first time since release were troubled by the chaplain's comments. I offered an alternative approach, with the chaplain still sitting in the room; but it was clear that they had been shaken.

Dan, a white, middle-aged businessman, told everyone, including the chaplain, that he had served two years in federal prison and that he was released more than fifteen years ago. He had completed parole almost twelve years ago. After orientation, we received a memo from the chaplain saying that Dan's application had been denied: "Not approved . . . Recent and serious Federal charges." The conviction was not recent, and he had not only completed his sentence but also met all other requirements. He has been "off paper"—no requirements for supervision or reporting for more than eleven years. Dan writes:

> If there is anyone qualified to speak to the issues facing current and former offenders, with all due respect, it is me. I not only know of the criminal justice system, but I have been through it, come out on the other side, and have never returned. I have been the recipient of forgiveness, grace, and restoration from my Creator. . . . No one knows better than me what it takes and what I went through to get to where I am—a place where every offender can be if he or she can receive the support necessary to help achieve restoration, to once again believe in themselves, to have the courage and willingness to be the person they really are. No one should ever be defined by their felony conviction.

When is the sentence completed? For most people, serving time inside a prison is a life sentence. The collateral damage continues for years. Dan noted that the chaplain's words during orientation put him back sixteen years—a prisoner defined by his crime, a number inside a dehumanizing system. Dan was eventually allowed to be a partner in the course, but it was not without incurring new wounds and experiencing a resurfacing of the old wounds. And it took going to high-level administrators to make it happen.

Breaking through barriers includes reckoning with the damage done by the system itself to those who serve time. As Harmon Wray and Laura Magnani write, the prison system creates mental and physical illness but offers minimal access to medical and mental-health services.[8] Anthony has had severe headaches for two years, but the only response has been to send him to the clinic to try a new medicine—no tests and no examination by a physician. Lenny has been incarcerated thirteen years for possession of drugs but has never had access to a substance-abuse treatment program. Antonio was diagnosed with mental illness as a teenager and required medication during high school. Incarcerated for more than eleven years now, he has never seen a psychiatrist or been given access to medications that might treat his illness.

Don Beisswenger, ordained clergy, retired seminary professor, and social-justice activist committed to nonviolence, served six months in federal prison for his witness against the School of the Americas. This is a man who carefully prepared and planned for his time in prison, a man who practices spiritual disciplines and is part of a supportive community. He received many letters and frequent visits while he was in prison and was able to afford the absurdly expensive collect phone calls home. And yet, he speaks often of the damage he experienced in the prison system—the confusion, vulnerability, disorientation, and depression that came as a result of relentless harassment and dehumanization, the demands for conformity and obedience to an endless list of rules that are enforced arbitrarily.[9]

Terry often begins the semester by telling people how much time he has served: "Hi, my name is Terry and this is my 12,164th day behind prison walls." More than thirty-two years in prison for a rape he committed when he was twenty-two. It was a crime of force and fear and violation and brutality of sexual violence. He was the first in his family to go to college. Except he came home—and raped a woman. He believes that his crime killed his mother. She died about two years after he was convicted and sent to prison, knowing that he would be gone a long time. He could not go home when she became ill or be there for the funeral. He loved his mother fiercely and talks about her often. He dreams of being home with his father, who is almost ninety and has several serious health problems. His father is determined to get Terry home before he dies.

Terry was one of the five original inside students for our Riverbend class. He loves to learn and write; engage in critical, creative thinking; and figure out how to apply what we learn. He is passionate and funny, witty and prophetic. He also struggles with depression. Although he takes antidepressants, maintaining a balance inside the walls after so many years is not easy. In his thirtieth year of continuous prison, he was placed on suicide watch. They moved him from his guild to a tiny isolation cell in the lockdown mental-health unit. He was given a bare mattress, paper gown, and paper slippers. No other clothes, no blanket, no books, no shower. When Harmon and I finally got to see him, we were shocked. We stood outside in the hall, trying to look through the pie-flap opening in the metal door of his cell. The opening is just big enough for our fingers to reach through so we could touch Terry's hand on the other side. Peeking through the opening, we wondered how healing is possible in such a barren place.

Prisons are the largest mental-health institutions in our country; and mental-health care, like healthcare in general, is inadequate, sporadic, and often dangerously inaccessible. Terry has no regular contact with either a psychological counselor or a psychiatrist. On one visit, the chaplain lets us borrow a folding chair he uses so that we could actually sit outside the locked metal door and peer into the pie flap, instead of squatting down or sitting on the floor.

"Please," Terry urged us, "Would you ask them to give me back my glasses and my Bible? They've taken them both away." Tears, prayers, and deep, shattering sobs. On another occasion, he pled: "Take my ring and give it to my father." We refused, knowing that this is the only thing he has left that reminds him of a life that used to be. "Please," he said, "I want to die. Just let me go." But we kept coming, knowing that we don't have the right words or much in the way of solutions; but we love Terry, and presence matters.

Not long after that visit, however, the mental-health staff in the lockdown unit decided to isolate Terry even more by preventing him from having any visitors—no pastors, family, or friends. "Isolation for mental-health reasons," we were told by the nurse. We tried to argue that cutting someone off from pastoral care, from family and friends is a cruel and unusual punishment, but no one seemed to listen. We called the state department of mental health, correctional staff, and other psychiatrists; but no one intervened.

Terry survived and was eventually moved back into the population. He has been a part of the prison classes every semester. When it is time for his parole hearing, lots of people are supportive. Terry is nervous, as are most people in that situation. Parole hearings are hard. They require a big commitment of time from folks on the outside. Outsiders have to be there to check in before things start, but one never knows when the case will be called or how long the hearing will take, or if a hearing officer will actually show up for the hearing. It is not uncommon to arrive at 7:45 A.M. and still be waiting at 2 P.M.

People on the inside both hope for and dread parole hearings. Sometimes there are people in the community who come to protest parole for a particular person. Sometimes no one is willing or able to be there to provide support or to testify on a prisoner's behalf and so he or she faces the situation alone. One never knows which hearing officer one will get, and there is often a huge difference in attitude between one hearing officer and the next. For some family members or loved ones who do come, this will be the first time to hear details of the crime; since so many insiders were convicted through plea bargaining, not trials. Most inmates want so much to be a new person, to leave that old person behind. Many want to reckon with the harm they have done, make amends where possible, and trust that there is life waiting on the other side. Parole hearings drag prisoners into their past.

Terry's parole hearing was astonishing from the start. Two correctional officers took time off work in order to testify for Terry. They have known him for most of his time inside; and they talked about his friendship, his genuine goodness, his gentleness, his advocacy for others inside the prison, and his willingness to work with almost anyone. Seminary students and professors, pastors and church friends, his father and his counselor all showed up. Never have I seen more supportive people at a parole hearing. No one was there to protest his release. But the hearing was over quickly. The hearing officer declared: "Due to the seriousness of your crime, I cannot recommend parole." Terry's father began to cry.

They took Terry back to his cell. The rest of us moved back to the visiting gallery, the hearing officer's decision clear to anyone who saw us. At this point, several others were crying. How much punishment is enough? What good comes from locking someone up for more than thirty years? The seriousness of his crime will never change. What are we waiting for?

Apocalyptic Acts: Unveiling Hidden Gifts, Creating Alternatives

The shift in social location, from center to margins, from power over to partnership with, from distance to proximity, is central to the biblical story. Consciously changing location is an apocalyptic act[10]—it unveils, reveals new truths, startling us so that we might recognize the ways in which we have "settled in as kept chaplains of an unjust order."[11] We discover anew the ways in which we have been seduced by "empire"—the prevailing society's ideology and theology; how we have been seduced with such power that we are no longer able to see or think beyond these narrow definitions of reality.[12]

One of the hardest barriers to overcome is the common definition of prison ministry as the good people from churches coming inside to minister to, evangelize, and "save" the lost people behind prison bars. This approach often silences the voices and hides the faces and stories of those on the inside and "forces others to inhabit your version of their reality."[13] In addition, it focuses the pastoral-care lens on the individual who is incarcerated, instead of on the systems and structures that have relentlessly pushed a larger and larger percentage of people from impoverished communities, especially communities of color, into the criminal justice system. The Bible reminds us that sin is structural and collective, not simply individual. The tendency among mainline denominations to remove the gospel from the margins distorts our understanding of Jesus, sin, salvation, and who the church is called to be. As Virgilio Elizondo writes:

> There is something in the colonized identity of the Galilean that people who have never been colonized do not suspect. There is something which the poor and exploited, the broken and the humiliated, the ridiculed and separated of the world have perceived that the powerful of this world have missed.[14]

Brazilian educator Paulo Freire defines the conscientization process as a communal dialogue that awakens people to rename the world through their own experience, recognizing both the powers that oppress, control, limit, and destroy and the powers of life and liberation, the possibilities for communal movement toward freedom.[15] This approach comes from a conviction that the people with the problems are the people with the solutions; that the most undereducated, impoverished, and struggling human beings bring gifts for analyzing the world in which they live in order to identify how they might move toward the world for which they yearn. And most often, they can name the powers and principalities at work in their world with more accuracy and prophetic honesty than can the parish clergy, bishops, folks in seminaries, or congregational leaders.

Inevitably, the classes and this long-term, mutual, open, and honest community inside the prison pull the veil off the myths and stereotypes perpetuated by the criminal justice system and our culture. It is not long into the conversation before it becomes very clear that the system is marked by race and class bias. While it is usually a surprise for outsiders, insiders know that who you are and where you come from make all the difference in the world as to how you will fare in the system. They also see more clearly who benefits and who is harmed by the way crime is defined in this country.

Building community takes time; although it always startles me to see how quickly the walls come down most of the time. A recent semester at the Annex was harder. There was significant tension around race. We were pleased to have had a larger group of white insiders than we had had before, but we soon discovered that several came with bad attitudes. We were not sure why they applied to participate or why they were approved, but there they were. During our first class, they refused to mingle, sticking instead to their White group. Even after being instructed to create diverse small groups, five White insiders refused to move. The next week they complained about the readings—"Incarceration has nothing to do with race. That's just hype; folks whining and complaining, and we're tired of it."

After class, the leadership team talked about the struggle. Do we ask them to leave, for the sake of the larger community? What does it mean to tolerate their racist behavior? What does it mean to challenge it? Jahi, a large Black man and a Muslim, who has been inside for more than twenty-nine years and who is part of our leadership team, responded: "This stuff is taught. It can be untaught. I got it. Just give me some time. We can do this."

And they did. The leadership team members on the inside kept on talking with, listening to, sharing with the White inmates who seemed so closed. They worked on loving those sharp edges into community. About halfway through the semester, one of the White insiders spoke up: "I want to apologize for all that stuff I've been writing and saying. I'm not really like that. I'm better than that. I can be. I will be. Thanks for giving me another chance." After two more weeks, he and Jahi were standing together laughing. "I see you." "I am here."

Shift to Riverbend, the maximum-security prison. We start the semester as usual—going around the circle, offering up first names and reasons for joining the class. We reminded participants that we were not asking anyone to disclose why he was in prison, any more than we would ask outsiders to share the worst thing they've done. Folks smiled, and we began.

I suspect that it was because Phil's case had been on the news that day: another priest arrested for sexual abuse. So reporters dragged up Phil's case all over again—a Roman Catholic priest convicted of molesting several teenaged boys. In introducing himself Phil often remarks that he is the only one in the class who really belongs behind bars. But this time he spoke about the classes he had attended before, prompted, I am sure, by his sense that, because of the news coverage, everyone now knows why he was there and what he had done.

About two-thirds of the way through the semester Phil mentioned something about his crimes, clearly thinking that everyone knew. But Laura hadn't known, and she was shocked. Laura and Phil had become friends over the past weeks. They often shared similar responses to the readings and sat next to each other, joking, telling stories, and sharing insights. Laura, a local pastor in her forties and a divorced mother of two teenaged boys, was going through the ordination process and finishing seminary.

Laura asked to talk with me after class. We sat in my parked car, watching rain stream down the windows. She started the conversation with a question about the assignment but then began to cry, sharing her story of abuse experienced as a child and the struggles she has gone through to find healing. She had sworn that she would never be in the same room with someone who had sexually abused children. But there she was in the classroom, suddenly comprehending this truth about her friend Phil. She looked up after hearing his words, expecting to see a monster; but it was only Phil. And she wondered whether this might be a sign of God's healing, a sign that she had moved through some wall and found new possibilities for her life. She told me about the years of therapy she had gone through to try to reckon with the many broken pieces of her heart and body. In the middle of her tears, she began to laugh: Wouldn't it be something if after all she had tried, she found healing in the prison?

I suggested that she go back to her therapist to talk through this experience. Did it make sense for her to continue the class? Would she feel safe? What might be danger signals she should watch for if she decided to continue coming? She did. She came back wanting to talk with Phil. She thought that he could help her move through some of the pain and deep scars; and she had worked with her therapist to make sure that it was a safe conversation. I suggested that she begin by writing to Phil so that he would have time to think and respond.

Phil was unnerved and edgy and not sure that this was a good idea. But the possibility that he might contribute to healing pushed him through his reservations. He was open and honest and responded to Laura's questions and ideas.

After some time, she requested to meet with Phil in person outside of class. In fact, she wanted to design some kind of healing liturgy for herself and ask Phil to participate. I said that I would explore the possibilities and asked her to go back to her therapist to concretely define both a plan and a safety net. I talked with Phil. He bordered on the edge of panic; but he said that he would do whatever was asked of him, grateful for an opportunity to contribute to good.

I made the arrangements for the three of us to meet in the chaplain's office. Laura had asked that she be allowed to bring water, one large bowl, and two smaller bowls. She had heard a story about pouring pain into the heart of God, the only heart large enough to hold so much hurt. She wanted to pour her pain into that large bowl and invite Phil to do the same. But the officials refused Laura's request. We were lucky to get fifteen minutes.

As we began, all of us were a bit nervous, including the chaplain. He kept interrupting the conversation to talk about irrelevant issues such as surveys and new forms. And then the storm came.

In a maximum-security prison, electrical storms mean lockdown. You stay where you are until the lightning stops. In case of a power outage, no doors, gates, or cells are to be left open. So everyone stays put until the storm passes. This particular storm lasted a while, with plenty of lightning and thunder. As the three of us sat there, locked in, we discovered that each of us had brought something with us. Phil had found two plastic lids and a larger bottle cap. On his way to the chaplain's office, he had asked for a cup of water; so now we had two small containers with water and a larger something to catch it when poured. Laura brought three tiny porcelain fish from her time in Japan. I brought three small wooden stars to remind us of God's light and God's invitation to us to be sources of light and life.

Laura and Phil waded in—talking, reading Scripture and litanies, sharing, singing, praying. The priest who would never be a priest again led us through a liturgy of healing and was invited to lay hands on one who had sworn she would never be in the same room with, let alone ever be touched by, someone who had molested children. It was an extraordinary moment, a holy time. What happened in that room could not be locked up. It could not be imprisoned or contained. God broke through all the barriers.

At the end, Phil started laughing. He told us about the priestly ritual of dipping an evergreen branch into water then sprinkling the water into the congregation. He used to delight in making sure that he flung water onto those who were trying to avoid getting wet. "God is making sure everyone is splashed with grace this night!" The rain stopped and the door opened. Phil went back to his guild, and Laura and I returned to our car. But the moment changed forever how we see one another and how we understand healing and grace.

Communal Pastoral Care: Resistance to Oppression

There is an African proverb that declares: "Because we are, I am. I am because we are." This proverb places the roots of individual identity in community and underlines the difficulty of finding our place in the world if we are isolated, disconnected, segregated, and separated. Pastoral care becomes a communal event, the creation and nurturing of "belongingness."[16] As Edward Wimberly notes in his writing on pastoral care in the Black church tradition, the dominant culture's tendency to focus on one-to-one therapy is a luxury in oppressed communities:

> To learn the methods and skills of the one-to-one healing model requires economic resources and extensive clinical and educational opportunities to which many black pastors did not have access until recently. . . . The black church had to rely upon a tradition of sustaining and guiding fashioned in response to oppression . . . finding corporate and communal means to meet the needs of persons when theoretical models were inadequate.[17]

Communal pastoral care requires uncovering the gifts and resources of the entire community in order to address hurts and struggles of individuals and to engage the systems and structures that cause the harm. This communal care embodies *ubuntu*—connectedness, a web of interrelatedness.[18] It stands in contrast to the more common and traditional approach that "isolates the individual from family, social, and economic contexts, thus ignoring the importance of relationships and systems in both forming individuals and enabling them to change."[19]

Healing happens for both insiders and outsiders as community grows. It is a miracle in and of itself: the very idea of a safe space in the middle of the prison; and, within that safe space, an invitation for people to really be themselves. People are often "listened into life."[20] So many good gifts are hidden behind prison walls. If it were not for the clothes, it might be hard to tell insiders from outsiders. Here are snapshots of this communal healing-from-the-inside-out from a recent semester:

White, middle-aged woman locked up for a short time on a charge of drunk driving: She was not involved in an accident and wasn't speeding. She was stopped for a broken taillight, during which she was tested for alcohol. She knows the shame, the humiliation, the dehumanization, the fear. She remembers the women inside the jail and the way several of them took care of her, comforting her, knowing that she was new to it all. She told no one at work, scared that she might lose her job. Nor did she tell her family or her church, worried that they would think less of her, judge her, even exclude her. There, in that class, she will share this story out loud for the first time. "*Sawabona.* I see you." "*Sikona.* I am here."

Young African-American male honorably discharged from the military after service in the Gulf War: He remained haunted by images of that war, troubled by his role in the killing and by his country's actions. He had almost made it through college when he was picked up on a first-time drug offense. He had no previous arrest record; and no weapons or violence were involved in the offense. Home is almost 400 miles away; so he has had no visitors. He comes to class, quiet and shy but excited for the opportunity to study, read, and engage others in critical thinking and dialogue. He is hungry for community, for a second chance, to be seen for something more than his crime. *Sawabona. Sikona.*

Young Latino male: He laughed when he discovered that someone in the class spoke Spanish, since he hadn't heard his mother tongue in many months. He struggled with English, telling us that he could not find words in English to describe what has happened to him and the complete isolation he felt. During those two hours in class, he said, he can come home to himself. *Usted veo. Soy aqui.* "I see you." "I am here."

An African-American male, entered the criminal justice system at age fifteen, now celebrating his fifty-second birthday: He has no family waiting—didn't have one when he came in at fifteen. Inside the prison walls he found a family and a community; and he learned something of the meaning of love. He is scared to go back out, having a hard time even imagining what that waiting world is like. Will people in this community really be family for him when he gets out? Can you see me? I am here.

An African-American female, late thirties, single mom working at a grocery store and going to school full time: She remembers being locked up, the shame and humiliation, the guards' harassment, and the strip searches. "Hurts to even think about it but that's why I had to come back inside. I know what it's like. . . . I had to tell my kids to keep it to themselves—so scared that teachers would write them off if they knew their mom was in jail; scared they'd be taken away. As Jahi said, you don't do time alone. Your family serves that time with you. And for what? Locked up for not paying parking tickets and then driving on a license that had been revoked because I couldn't pay the parking tickets. Still don't have the money to pay. Still have to get in that car in order to get to work in order to earn the money so I can try to pay these fines that keep adding up, getting bigger. Sometimes it feels like there's no way out. It's a crime to be poor in this country, and you know that I'm right about that."

An African American male, high-level administrator: "I don't see myself as all that dissimilar from people on the inside. . . . One time I heard that we were having problems with one of our treatment facilities, so I had myself referred there as a client. They had no idea who I was. In the intake interview, they kept asking: 'Why are you here? What were you doing?' I responded: 'I was just standing on the corner.' 'Well,' they were quick to reply, 'you shouldn't have been standing on that corner, should you?' And it reminded me of the history of jump and grabs in West Tennessee. At harvest time, they'd jump out and grab folks, dragging them in and forcing them to work the fields at harvest time. I was just struck by the fact that it's the same now—jump and grab—in urban settings. . . . We've managed to criminalize so many things in America."

"As Beautiful as a Yes in a Room Full of No's"

This chapter has attempted to close the distance between inside and outside, to identify a path through the barriers, to uncover the power of community defined by partnership and mutuality, and the resulting collective movement to engage systems and structures in ways that promote healing and wholeness, justice and transformation. One high-level administrator uses the word *habilitation* instead of *rehabilitation*, noting that one cannot restore what never was. He argues that the societal safety net has failed those who are incarcerated—Black and White, male and female, young and old:

> The net failed—whether it is education or jobs, treatment for the mentally ill or for people caught up in alcohol and drugs. The net failed. In some cases, people have been let down by churches. I want to create the opportunities for people to hear the voices inside, to acknowledge the humanity in everyone.

Ninety-five percent of those on the inside are eventually returned to communities on the outside. While recidivism rates are high, most of the charges are technical violations, not new crimes. Transformation and Reconciliation from the Inside Out (TRIO), a think tank and action team that grew out of our Inside Out classes, works with congregations to design reentry support teams. Insiders who have graduated from the class and been released become leaders in this work. The affirmation of their gifts and somebodiness continues, as they give back to the community. This is communal pastoral care: we hold one another and we hold one another accountable.[21]

Kahuna, serving a long sentence at Riverbend, was taken by our focus on restorative justice. He received permission from the warden to write letters to his victim. For two years he wrote letters attempting to make amends, to apologize, praying for good for the person he had harmed. For two years there was no response. Then one day the letter came. Not too many months after that, the victim came to visit him at Riverbend—and to forgive him. "I stood tall that day, and I've been living ever since."

Mustafa, quiet, steady, gentle, and consistently responsible, has been a part of the leadership team. Recently he was put on work release and now is going home. On his last night in prison, he stood in the middle of our circle and said thanks: "This class helped me believe I could make it. It helped me see I am somebody and not to be so ashamed. But it's scary out there. I'd get to thinking everyone knew I was a criminal. I'd try to make myself small. Be real quiet. Not look at people. Then this man comes up to me the other day and shakes my hand. Not like you do when you feel sorry for someone but like you do when you're meeting a real person, like we do in here. And he tells me I'm doing a good job and would I like to work with him. And I felt something in myself. Something good. I remembered my family here. I gotta tell you, if I can make it, anyone can."

Zahir was released from the Annex and soon enrolled as a student at American Baptist College, where I teach. When the semester started, he came back inside the prison as an outsider who was working full time and going to school full time. He was a walking sign of hope. Every week, his presence reminded people that they too could make it on the outside. In the prison compound, a line drawn on the concrete walkway near the exit marks off prisoners from outsiders. All goodbyes must be made on the inside of the line. On the first night of reentering the prison as an outsider, completing class and getting ready to leave, Zahir came to the line: "Wait. Remember all those times I had to stop here? I told you, one day I'd walk out of here with you, one day I'd cross that line. Watch!" And he walked across the line. Insiders and outsiders celebrated as grace was made visible and hope grew larger.

Dorothee Soelle quotes a poem written by Joao Cabral: "He is as beautiful as a Yes in a room full of No's . . . Beautiful because he is a door that turns into many exits." And then she goes on: "To love life . . . where it has been condemned to death, even from its very beginning, is an old human ability to go beyond what is. That ability is called transcendence or faith or hope—or listening to the silent cry. It is the most important movement that human beings can learn in their lives."[22]

Pastoral care *with*—not *to* or *for*—people caught up inside the prison system requires focusing on a healing process through community. Observes one high-level administrator in the correctional system:

> Congregations have got to facilitate healing, a process of making the victim and victimizer whole. Go in with eyes wide open, knowing healing happens one day at a time—not just that one time they come forward in a church service. . . . Build realistic

partnerships with the criminal justice system. . . . Offer up
opportunities based on the possibility of making a change.

Pastoral care requires mobilizing the resources of the entire community to address the harm and create possibilities for reconciliation
and transformative justice. It begins with this authentic partnership
over time that redefines our understanding of the criminal justice
system, opens our eyes, ears, and hearts, and empowers us to see and
be seen. This ongoing encounter in community mobilizes us to confront the systems and structures that diminish life, to work collectively for concrete changes to policies, and to "decriminalize
behavior that involves homelessness, mental illness, drug addiction,
or consensual sex between adults."[23] It empowers us to challenge
zero-tolerance policies for children; educational systems that dump
more than half of our high-school students onto the streets, without
any certificate or degree; a social-service system that abandons people to poverty; and a criminal justice system that is locking up children at a younger and younger age. "*Sawabona*. I see you." *Sikona*. I
am here."

Afterword

As I was finishing the manuscript for this chapter, I learned that
Harmon Wray had died suddenly. It was, and still is, a shock. Harmon
was a theologian, an advocate, an agitator, and a wild and wonderful
prophet and friend. For more than thirty years, he was family for
many behind prison walls. He wrote the United Methodist Women's
mission book on restorative justice[24] and headed up that office for
the brief time it existed. When he died, Richard Goode and I started
making phone calls to the prison so that we could share the news
with the inside students. Some had been in every class since that first
one in January 2003. Many had known Harmon for a long time. We
thought that people needed to be able to grieve together as we had
been doing at the hospital, to be community with one another, to
share stories and sorrow.

Judy, Harmon's first love for more than thirty-five years, announced that she was going with us. "No," we responded, pastoral care professionals cautioning her to take care of herself at this moment. "You haven't slept. People are still coming to see you here at the hospital. They haven't taken Harmon for the transplant surgery, and you still have decisions to make. It makes no sense for you to come." "I'm coming," she declared. "Harmon is not in that hospital room. He is already dead. And if he is anywhere, I suspect he's already at the prison. So I'm going with you."

And she did. It was an extraordinary and holy time. So many tears. Such deep grief. Sitting together, not sure what to do. Judy started: "I had to be here because Harmon carried you with him all the time. He loved you so, and you loved him." An astonishing pastoral moment for everyone involved. Tears shared inside the prison, a not-common event inside these walls. Folks made vulnerable in their grief and opening themselves in this safe space. Stories. Deep sadness in people who so rarely experience the unconditional long-term loving that Harmon offered. "He identified with us," someone said. "He saw us as real people." "Harmon donated a piece of himself for us and it will be with me always." "I get Jesus now, because of Harmon. He showed me what forgiveness looks like when it walks in a human being."

At Harmon's memorial celebration, I offered a prayer that included these words: "And now, O God, I pray that you would not only comfort us, but that you would also disturb us and anoint us with your Spirit. Send us back into the world to live with the same kind of vision and holy boldness that we celebrate in Harmon. Allow his life and witness to challenge and change us so that we, too, might invest everything in out-loud loving, so that we too might agitate and advocate, organize and strategize, reconcile and redeem, companion and comfort, trouble and transform until all the chains are broken, all the prison doors opened and your justice flows down like a mighty river." May it be so.

NOTES

1. Martin Luther King, Jr., called Reverend James Lawson, a United Methodist pastor now teaching at Vanderbilt University, the "leading nonviolence theorist in the world."

2. After nine semesters, A.J. Levine, a New Testament scholar at Vanderbilt Divinity School, became the first full-time professor to schedule a course at Riverbend. She has been present every semester since then. Other professors have included Douglas Knight, Professor of Hebrew Bible; and Ray Waddle, adjunct professor and religion editor of the *Tennessean* newspaper. I am working with Margaret Atkins and Drew University Theological School to expand this model in partnership with insiders who are Rising Hope graduates at Arthur Kill Correctional Institution. The Drew courses will be offered through two New Jersey prisons beginning in Fall 2008.

3. Lori Pompa, Temple University, developed the Inside Out Prison Exchange Program through a partnership with the Lifers Group at Graterford Prison near Philadelphia. I attended their first national training and came back to work with Glenda Lingo, coordinator of the Parents in Prison program (and a most wonderful sister, who helped with this chapter and the rest of my life). We designed and implemented the first Inside Out program in the southeast. Lori's national training network has now trained more than 100 people from 80 colleges and universities in more than 30 states.

4. World Council of Churches Central Committee, "Being Church and Overcoming Racism: It's Time for Transformative Justice" (26 August–3 September, 2002): "In the context of racial-ethnic justice, churches, governments, civil society, victims or offenders cannot restore—*reinstate, re-establish, bring back, return*—what has been lost. . . . Transformative justice deals with the past in the present. Its goal is to overcome racism and achieve healing, reconciliation and the re-establishment ('to put relationship right') of people's relationship with a particular focus on *justice* to racially and ethnically oppressed peoples." Available online: *http://www2.wcc-coe.org/ccdocuments.nsf/index/plen-4-en.html.*

5. See Pamela Couture, *Seeing Children, Seeing God: A Practical Theology of Children and Poverty* (Nashville: Abingdon, 2000), 56.

6. Since 1981 New York Theological Seminary has offered an intensive 36-credit Master of Professional Studies designed for long-term prisoners in New York state correctional facilities.

7. Most inmates in Tennessee prisons earn 17 cents per hour. Work-release inmates must pay $485 per month in rent for staying in the bunk-bed dorm of the prerelease prison.

8. Harmon Wray and Laura Magnani, *Beyond Prisons: Our New Interfaith Paradigm for Our Failed Prison System* (Minneapolis: Fortress, 2006), 100, 122–26.

9. Don Beisswenger, *Locked Up: Letters and Papers of a Prisoner of Conscience* (Nashville: Upper Room Books, 2008).

10. Thanks to Richard Goode for this insight and for help with this chapter.

11. The phrase belongs to Walter Wink.

12. Walter Brueggemann, *The Prophetic Imagination* (Minneapolis: Augsburg Fortress, 2001), 126–30.

13. Philip Gourevitch, *We Wish to Inform You that Tomorrow We Will Be Killed with Our Families: Stories from Rwanda* (New York: Picador, 1999), 181.

14. Virgilio Elizondo, *A God of Incredible Surprises: Jesus of Galilee* (Lanham: Rowman and Littlefield, 2003), 5. Used by permission.

15. Paulo Freire, *Pedagogy of the Oppressed* (New York: Continuum International Publishing Group, 2000).

16. J. Deotis Roberts, quoted in Toinette Eugene and James Newton Poling, *Balm in Gilead: Pastoral Care for African American Families Experiencing Abuse* (Nashville: Abingdon, 1998), 25.

17. Edward P. Wimberly, *Pastoral Care in the Black Church* (Nashville: Abingdon, 1979), 22–23; quoted in Eugene and Poling, *Balm in Gilead*, 155.

18. Eugene and Poling, *Balm in Gilead*, 186–89.

19. Wray and Magnani, *Beyond Prisons*, 159.

20. Marsha Foster Boyd, "WomanistCare: Some Reflections on the Pastoral Care and the Transformation of African American Women," in *Embracing the Spirit: Womanist Perspectives on Hope, Salvation and Transformation*, ed. by Emilie Townes (Maryknoll, NY: Orbis, 1997), 200.

21. Retired United Methodist bishop Kenneth Carder made this point in a sermon several years ago.

22. From *The Silent Cry*, by Dorothee Soelle, copyright © 2001 Fortress Press, 282. Used by special permission of Augsburg Fortress Publishers.

23. Wray and Magnani, *Beyond Prisons*, 163.

24. Harmon Wray, *Restorative Justice: Moving Beyond Punishment* (New York: General Board of Global Ministries, The United Methodist Church, 2002).

CHAPTER 8

Returning to the Fold—But to What?

DALLAS TERRELL

Most incarcerated persons will eventually return to family, neighborhood, and community, too often with devastating results. Many will not be restored and will return to prison. Children, spouses, parents, and families (both core and nuclear) frequently miss out on restored relationships. Victim and offender most often do not experience amendatory and restorative contacts. This chapter addresses the difficult issues of reentry and restoration of prisoners to the community. I examine the multitude of needs, problems, and situations associated with maintaining vital relationships between the offended and the offenders and with spouses and families while incarcerated and during the long trip back home. The plight of persons released from incarceration, the stress of their families on the outside, and building and maintaining constructive patterned relationships—all are aspects of the discussion below.

There is plenty of conversation about the plight of the ex-offender and his or her family as they learn to deal with having the family member back in their lives. Some people concentrate on the feelings and situations of those who are released and their immediate and extended families' experiences. The following excerpts, based on interviews and communication with family members, actual offenders, and workers on various sides of the dynamics of reentry, speak to critical aspects that need to be addressed in forging a better tomorrow for offender, ex-offender, and family.

> Returning to the fold won't be easy on either side, not for the one returning nor for the one who has always been there. It won't be easy.

> Expectations will be everywhere. The expectation that the one returning, or "returnee," must do better will stare everyone in the face, creating a blanket of anxiety all around. The expectation that the one who has always been there, or the "waitee," just will not accept the returnee and move on with life will be an undercurrent that can eat away at progress.

> Understanding compromise on both sides is imperative. But it is not, will never be, a fifty-fifty proposal. Although love is the premier element in the lives of humankind, trust between those involved must be the focal point in establishing a new relationship. And a new relationship is required, for the old one offers nothing good.

> The "returnee" has the burden of proof to demonstrate a change of lifestyle—attitude, habits, desires, needs, etc.—showing a transition to a "better" person. Therefore, the one returning will always be on the short end of the compromise stick, seemingly forever giving more than receiving. For this to work, the "I'm-not-able-to-do-this, I'm-not-able-to-do-that" attitude won't cut it. There must exist an attitude of "let-me-find-something-I-can-do-so-I-can-prove-my-worth" that is demonstrated by actions and fruitful results. Sitting on one's duff, waiting for life (and others) to do for you just will not produce a successful outcome.

> The "waitee" has the burden of proof of willingness to try. But trying can be a difficult thing when offers of help are constantly

rejected. No matter that the one offering and the one refusing don't see eye-to-eye, if the item offered hurts no one and possibly helps some, the rejection of that offer eventually erodes any willingness to "be there" for the "returnee." However, one must not confuse willingness to try with meekness. They are not the same. Meekness will forever allow the returnee to carry on with only a surface show of transition. Willingness to try requires a deep, positive transition that radiates from the core of the returnee. The returnee is seeking to get where the "waitee" is, and beyond. (Perhaps that is why the understanding compromise will never be a fifty-fifty proposition.)

Continuous confusion of meekness with willingness eventually results in the "returnee" and associated needs/desires becoming non-existent to the "waitee."[1]

Dazara Ware of the Metro Transition Center in Atlanta, Georgia, was passionate as she provided her thoughts on persons returning to the community. Issues of trust, self-encouragement, alienation, and determination, she says, loom large as determinants of how well persons reentering the family after incarceration will succeed. She points out that the issue of trust is an undercurrent for both the family and the previously incarcerated person, especially as those involved struggle to maintain a lifestyle that will be acceptable to all. Ms. Ware is adamant that both the ex-offender and the family have "done time." Although in different physical surroundings, everyone shared the "hell." And the issues extend beyond the immediate family to include: lack of good sleep because of questions about the real intentions of the ex-offender, financial concerns around adequate housing and sufficient food, adequate care of minor children, and more. She counsels the women at the Metro Atlanta Transition Center to have a plan, because "If there is no plan, the plan is to fail."[2]

A young female first offender on probation and with no record of conviction addresses the difficulties surrounding being unable to find a job because of her crime.

A second chance is needed for persons who are first-time offenders and on probation. People with children, like me, need jobs other than the minimum wages associated with most fast-food type jobs that are available. This will help us become all that we can be and prevent our becoming a burden on our families. Too often the punishment, with all of the time constraints, prevents good employment that provides for other necessities like housing, transportation, child care, food, clothing, etc.[3]

Denise Blake, President of SuccessSolutions and former Director of the Re-entry National Media Outreach Campaign, a program focused on the various aspects of life after incarceration, discusses the impact of incarceration on the various aspects of family life before and after release.

From my time of directing the Re-entry National Media Outreach Campaign, I learned of a number of coping strategies for families of a person in jail or prison. First is to let loose any feeling of stigma related to the incarceration of their loved one. At this point in America's history, virtually every man, woman, and child has someone close to them who is currently or has been in the criminal justice system. The incarceration of a loved one really has nothing to do with, and reflects neither positively nor negatively on, their family. It just happens. It happens to "rich" families, "poor" families, White ones, Black ones, and every type of family in between. Second, families don't need to cope alone. Investigate family support centers, houses of worship and other faith-based support organizations, and social services to learn more about resources to help alleviate the gap left by the incarcerated person. Third, think about the period post-incarceration. Will the loved one be returning to the home from which they left? I can't advocate any particular strategy, as each family situation is different, but there is the possibility to consider that the loved one cannot or should not return to the same situation. I suggest seeking counseling support to deal with any of the above scenarios.[4]

A police officer in New York offers these insights on the variety of issues that impact so many aspects of society as the entire community is forced to address the possibilities that affect the state of reentry, even from early childhood:

> Some people are born bad. No matter what you do they are set to be criminals. They are taught to cheat, steal, get over, etc. They grow up watching and learning how to beat the system, from welfare to social security to whatever system they can beat . . .
>
> In a society such as ours, we live in times where it's glorious to bring down the person whether male or female. Our schools play a major role; prenatal care plays a role, and so on and so on. When you have an individual who is or was incarcerated, whether overnight or for months or years, they learn a life behind those walls that teaches them bad. And I do mean *bad*! So when they are released into society it's as if the cards are stacked against them.
>
> Prisons are not places of rehabilitation as they should be. There are plenty of documented facts that once you are incarcerated you will be back. But once you reveal that you have been incarcerated, we have a way, or should I say, society has a way of turning up their noses at them. . . .
>
> America has a reputation for drugs and there is plenty of money involved which fuels another aspect of crime. God-fearing families don't want to believe that their flesh and blood of whatever relationship is bad and will ignore all signs when they display this behavior while they are young. It might be cheaper to get them some sort of counseling when they are young to possibly ward off any bad doings in life. By the age of 13 most children know if they want to do right or wrong.[5]

These various perspectives highlight some of the issues that must be addressed in order for both the ex-offender and his or her family to achieve a satisfying life and to avoid the pitfalls of recidivism and continued pain for the families. Issues such as the type of offense, probation requirements, and the age and sex of the client play an extremely important role in the lives of the ex-offender and his or her family. Many agencies across the United States seek to address the multitude of issues impacting the living situation of persons that are released with various stipulations for their continued "freedom."

The Hope Hall Foundation, an extension of the Fulton County Superior Court in Atlanta, Georgia, provides a structured program for persons convicted of drug-related crimes to prevent their returning to prison. During a regular meeting in May 2007, I spoke with family members and "clients," who shed light on yet more of the difficulties family members encounter upon release of an incarcerated family member. The group consisted of ten females and five males, with ages ranging from teens to sixty-three years, and included a recently released offender who had served eleven years as a result of crimes committed as a substance abuser and who is now serving as a mentor for an offender relative. The persons confirmed the litany of issues facing reentry: trust, health, difficulties finding employment, denial (by both ex-offender and family), probation requirements, and the impact of having multiple members in the reentry category.[6]

As is clear from these accounts, the process of reentry raises a complex set of issues that need careful consideration by everyone involved. In what follows, I select seven issues for more detailed examination: preparation for release, housing, employment, health, education, spiritual affirmation, and social adjustments.

Preparation for Release

It is critical that both the person being released and the community that will receive him or her prepare carefully to reduce the risk of recidivism and to make the transition as seamless as possible for everyone involved, particularly for the family. Not surprisingly, perhaps, such preparation varies considerably around the country, from virtually no effort in some communities to extensive processes in others. A carefully planned process that draws on a variety of resources—correctional institutions, church groups, community organizations, and private individuals—can make all the difference in addressing challenges and obstacles. I mention just a couple of examples.

Rev. Eugene Neville of the Mount Moriah Baptist Church saw the need to provide the children of incarcerated persons in Brockton, Massachusetts, a positive visitation environment to help reduce the pressures of children visiting their incarcerated fathers. Out of this need emerged a powerful partnership between churches, the state, and the community in Brockton. Rev. Neville and his church partnered with Weed and Seed, the Polycom Corporation, and the District Attorney's Office to provide video visitation with the fathers and their children, resulting in a significant decrease of stress for the children and preparation for the release of the father. "When they saw us reach out to their families," says Rev. Neville, "that meant something."[7]

The Offender Parolee Probationer State Training Employment Program (TOPPSTEP) is an innovative partnership between the State Board of Pardons and Paroles, the Department of Corrections, and the Department of Labor in Georgia. The program assists offenders returning to society by providing resource and support information, academic and vocational instruction, and job counseling. The latter includes resume writing, interview skills, job search, networking techniques, and placement services.[8]

Housing

The challenges in obtaining adequate housing are numerous for both the returnee and his or her family. I mention just a few:

- In many cases, the returnee's only option is to move back in with the family, which often exacerbates already-crowded living conditions.
- Restrictions placed on ex-felons generally prevent them from obtaining federally sponsored housing that would normally be available for someone faced with similar economic challenges.
- Limitations on income typically exclude ex-offenders from locating in nicer, more desirable neighborhoods.
- Aspects of the criminal justice system present significant hurdles, such as medical and financial assistance, for the returnee and his or her spouse and children.

Indeed, food stamps and cash benefits provided through Temporary Assistance for Needy Families (TANF) are routinely denied to former prisoners with a felony drug conviction.[9] Family members often are confronted with difficult choices about the kind of support they can provide and how long they can sustain it. Other issues, such as custody of grandchildren, schooling, clothing, church attendance, and social activities, often raise thorny problems, especially when the ex-offender parent resides in the same neighborhood or in the same home and has limited resources for taking care of the children. Restrictions on felons prevent spouses from obtaining housing that would be available under normal circumstances. What makes matters worse is that the issues I outlined above barely scratch the surface of the housing challenges facing ex-offenders and their families.

Employment

The ex-offender's opportunity to find sustainable employment is impacted by several factors, including his or her previous employment and educational level and the willingness of employers to give the formerly incarcerated another chance. While some states do offer transitional training, ex-felons still experience limits on their ability to find jobs. Indeed, for persons transitioning back into society the negative impact of their incarceration affects their total life, including their families.

A state parole officer in Northwestern Connecticut insists that too often a negative self-image on the part of ex-felons, particularly those who are undereducated and poorly trained, hinders their ability to find rewarding employment. Consequently, many turn to drugs, which negatively affects a successful return to life outside the prison walls.

Education

Many states offer incarcerated persons training to facilitate their return to the "outside." This assistance typically includes providing

GED classes, as well as undergraduate and professional-level programs. These efforts are designed to better prepare the offender (male and female of varying ages) for a new life in hopes that a better education will contribute to a more positive "after-prison" life.

The Re-entry National Media Outreach Campaign, funded by the Annie E. Casey Foundation, works across the United States to provide a variety of media resources that address various issues of prisoner reentry. A program called "Bridging the Gap: A Writing Workshop" responds to the increase of girls and women in prison. Under the guidance of Vicki Lopez, former Lee County, Florida, Commissioner, the program seeks to intervene in the lives of at-risk girls, teaching them about the consequences of their actions and preparing them for a new life on the outside.[10]

Health

It is generally accepted that HIV/AIDS and substance abuse are the major illnesses with which many incarcerated persons have to cope. However, research concludes that other sexually transmitted diseases, as well as mental-health disorders (including anger management), should be added to the list. While some facilities address most of the illnesses of the incarcerated, challenges following release often prevent a healthy lifestyle for many. Community health centers, the Veterans Health Administration, United Way, substance-abuse organizations, crisis help lines, and other community and faith-based groups offer various types of assistance to these individuals.

Such assistance is extremely important because most ex-felons find it very difficult to obtain health insurance. Indeed, the U.S. Department of Labor seeks to address some of these concerns through its Substance Abuse Mental Health Services/Center for Substance Abuse Prevention (SAMHSA/CSAP) grant. This grant provides funds for organizations with existing prisoner reentry programs that would benefit from parts of the grant, including healthcare.[11]

Spiritual Affirmation

Traditional ministry work with offenders involves counseling and reentry preparation; but the problems involved with family reunification are often overlooked or revealed only as problems surface. Additionally, because of varying faith traditions, considerations for persons' particular beliefs must be accounted for so as not to appear to disrespect or cross the lines of specific beliefs.

The complex circumstances facing ex-offenders and their families who are trying to make a better life often go unnoticed. As a result, the person sitting next to you in the pew could be experiencing a deep test of faith and you may never know it, because he or she does not want to "air his or her dirty laundry." Conversely, some persons may be very open about their situation—indeed, proud to tell their story. Usually, they are actively involved in the various activities the church offers.

Dr. Walter H. McKelvey, President-Dean of Gammon Theological Seminary at the Interdenominational Theological Center in Atlanta, Georgia, speaks to the importance of knowing when and at what level it is appropriate to get involved in the lives of persons in these situations.

> In my many years of ministry and service in The United Methodist Church, it has always been important to me to allow for where people are in their faith journey, while at the same time seizing every opportunity to provide assistance as the need is gleaned. I see this type of sensitivity as equally important for the member in the pew as well as for the pastoral staff. The ministries of our churches must be overarching to include as wide an array of needs as possible . . . counseling, employment, housing, clothing, childcare assistance, etc. We are all God's children and need to take care of our family members as best we can.[12]

Partnerships between the faith community and various community organizations provide effective ways to address many of the needs of persons seeking to move their lives forward after incarceration. The program developed by Rev. Eugene Neville in Brockton, Massachusetts, mentioned earlier, again is a good example. His church, the Weed and Seed site, the sheriff's office, and the parole office continue to discuss the status of the program and ideas for expanding it, such as discussing the need for housing for ex-offenders, searching for new income streams to provide continuous work, and more. Their dedication is clear: "We have to be committed, because we're dealing with people's lives."[13]

Social Adjustments

The social adjustments needed for a successful transition are deeply intertwined with answers to questions like these:

- "What am I going back to?"
- "Who is forgiving, and who is not?"
- "How do I deal with moving on and up with all of the restrictions forced on me?"
- "How do I dress right when I don't have any money?"
- "May I go to church? Whom do I talk to about this?"

Equally, many questions plague the family member:

- "What kinds of things should or should I not talk about?"
- "Do I have to give up some of my acquaintances?"
- "What do I do to keep my sanity when he goes off?"
- "How long will I have to support her?"

Dealing with these and other questions is most important and is an ongoing process. There is no "magic wand" for reentry that provides an instant cure; nor is there a solution that works exactly the same for each person. Both the "re-enterer" and family members need to be open to using the resources of an assortment of persons, agencies, corporations, and ministries that seek to facilitate their particular reentry process.

Conclusion

The challenge of facilitating reentry into a community one has aggrieved in the past looms large. As we have seen, the challenge is multifaceted, affecting the ex-offender/returnee, his or her family, and the receiving community.

Only by being acquainted with as many facets of the reentry process as possible, the "eyes wide open" acknowledgement of individual situations, and the reaching out to seek and provide assistance can the struggle be mitigated and the most beneficial solutions achieved. When all resources are used, the process of getting to the right place can be positive for everyone involved. How can people of faith find our places as we move to make the "crooked" paths straight . . . as we strive to alleviate the impact of incarceration and reentry on ex-offenders . . . and their families . . . on the way to our shared eternal home?

NOTES

1. Comment submitted by Dorothy Ann Turnipseed, family member of previously incarcerated person, 21 August 2007.

2. Interview with Dazara Ware, Metro Transition Center, Atlanta, Georgia, August, 2007.

3. Discussion with female on probation for first offense, August 2007.

4. Comment submitted by Denise Blake, former director of Re-entry National Media Outreach Campaign, August 2007.

5. Comment submitted by Alfred Woodall, veteran New York City police officer, August 2007.

6. Author's discussion with family members of Hope Hall Foundation in Atlanta, Georgia, May 2007.

7. Eugene Neville, Mt. Moriah Baptist Church, Brockton, Massachusetts, 2005 See *http://www.ncjrs.gov/ccdo/in-sites/spring2005/reentry_3.html*.

8. For more information on TOPPSTEP, visit *http://www.dcor.state.ga.us/Divisions/OPT/Reentry/index.html*.

9. Amy E. Hirsch, et. al., *Every Door Closed: Barriers Facing Parents with Criminal Records* (Washington, DC: Center for Law and Social Policy and Community Legal Services, Inc., 2002).

10. For more information, visit "Re-entry National Media Outreach Campaign" at *http://www.re-entrymediaoutreach.org.*

11. For more information about SAMHSA/CSAP, visit the website of the U.S. Department of Labor at *http://www.dol.gov.*

12. Comment submitted by Dr. Walter H. McKelvey, Gammon Theological Seminary, Atlanta, Georgia, August 2007.

13. Rev. Eugene Neville, Mt. Moriah Baptist Church. Brockton, Massachusetts, 2005. See *http://www.ncjrs.gov/ccdo/in-sites/spring2005/reentry_3.html.*

CHAPTER 9

Reclaiming Holistic Prison Ministry: Some Recommendations for Action

JAMES M. SHOPSHIRE, SR.; MARK C. HICKS; AND RICHMOND STOGLIN

We come now to the culmination of the effort to develop a renewed approach to prison and criminal justice ministry from a restorative justice perspective. Our intent has been to present perspectives concerning the field of criminal justice ministry, recall the connection of that ministry to the restorative grace of God, remember the Methodist heritage, and take stock of our recent history in prison ministry. A number of perspectives have been offered, and yet, while different, all are pertinent in the overarching socio-theology of responsive and responsible restorative justice for victims, offenders, and the communities out of which they come and to which they return.

The question now is, what is next? As United Methodists, what plan of action emerges for our ministry with the criminal justice system? How might we uphold the legacy and work of the Methodists into the future? How ought we to conduct ourselves in response to what God has done and is doing? How, as people restored by God's grace, can we purposefully act and live out patterns of restorative love in prisons and communities and in our lives and relationships?

To this end, this final chapter refers to a variety of approaches, plans of action, and resources for criminal justice ministry and prison ministry in The United Methodist Church. Each of the ministry communities—chaplains, congregational and community-based programs, and theological seminaries—will lift prospects for our future in ministry and offer recommendations for each ministry community as well as for the whole United Methodist Church.

Recommendations for Chaplains

Richmond Stoglin

As a former prison chaplain, I believe The United Methodist Church has to put thick rhetoric into thick action. Today, our greatest mission field is the prisons. As the *Book of Resolutions* reminds us, the incarcerated "is the most isolated, alienated and forgotten segment of our population and it is growing even as crime rates decrease."[1]

In his book *Race to Incarcerate*, Marc Maurer states: "Rather than looking for a political hero to lead us out of this wilderness, we would do better to consider how we might mobilize a greater constellation of forces to demand a more constructive approach."[2] The suggestions below, and in the rest of this chapter, aim to encourage such a "constellation of forces" among the people called United Methodists.

- Redouble the effort at recruiting, training, and equipping chaplains for ministry with the incarcerated. As I pointed out earlier, as of August 2007, there were only 36 United Methodist prison chaplains in the entire United States. Out of a total of nearly 300 chaplains, only six serve in the Bureau of Prisons. The remaining thirty serve in local jails and state prisons. Perhaps most troubling, there are no United Methodist juvenile justice chaplains anywhere in the United States (the last one retired in 2005). More must be done before juveniles grow into adult prisoners.

- Contribute to the only United Methodist prison scholarship fund in existence, the Coleman Tyson Siekman (CTS) Prison Chaplain Scholarship Endowment. The objective of the fund is to endow the scholarship with one million dollars in order to effectively recruit, retain, and support committed United Methodist persons called to full-time correctional ministry. To learn more about the endowment, visit The United Methodist Higher Education Foundation at *http://www.umhef.org.*
- Invite prison chaplains to preach, lead workshops, and help design study guides in criminal justice and prison ministry for use at all levels of the connection, from general agencies to local churches.
- Establish a national United Methodist prison ministry database to connect general agencies, local churches, experienced volunteers, and community resources in shared ministry.
- Encourage each recognized United Methodist caucus to add a section on prison ministry to its national mandate. Additionally, invite caucuses to include prison ministry as a regular feature of its national meeting agenda.
- Work to implement what the *Book of Resolutions* has outlined regarding the commitment of funds, staff, and construction of a Prison/Criminal Justice Ministry.[3] Through this concerted effort of church agency integration being intentionally focused on eliminating the growing prison-industrial complex the church will become stronger.
- Encourage the Council of Bishops to designate a bishop to serve as its correctional ministry representative, with the assignment of annually convening a consultation to review correctional/criminal justice issues and actions to ensure mutual accountability and demonstrate the church's commitment to this Wesleyan tradition.
- Begin churches devoted entirely to ministry with ex-offenders and their families. XOC (Ex-Offender Church), located in Lancaster, Pennsylvania, and part of the Eastern Pennsylvania Annual Conference, is an effective example of such a church. The mission of this unique church is to address the spiritual

needs of ex-offenders and their families. This ministry is partially sponsored by the General Board of Global Ministries and the Eastern Pennsylvania Annual Conference.

Recommendations for Congregations and Communities

Mark C. Hicks

Congregation/community-based ministry is a very important connective link within the overall gambit of prison ministry and criminal justice ministry. These communities engage inmates and chaplains on the inside of prisons, families and significant others during incarceration, and officials and former inmates after release from prison and as the latter begin reentry back into the community.

Ministers and congregations on the outside have the opportunity to address certain practices and systems through advocacy, engage in efforts of reform, and challenge corrupt and misguided ways of administering criminal justice programs. The church on the outside can also give impetus to changes in legislative and regulatory patterns that contradict the goals of restorative justice.

The people in our churches, both laity and clergy, have the best vantage point to help seminaries, annual conferences, boards of ordained ministry, and other agencies of the church to expand their understanding of the needs and issues in prison ministry and to reach for higher levels of involvement. I offer the following recommendations as ways to further this worthy goal.

- Create a criminal justice ministries academy whose aim is to promote restorative justice issues and to train church practitioners in various forms of criminal justice ministry. Hosted annually by one of our United Methodist seminaries for one or two weeks, the academy will feature lectures and workshops by noted experts in the field of restorative justice and criminal justice ministry.
- Require training in criminal justice ministry for all candidates for ordained ministry in The United Methodist Church.

Boards of ordained ministry can offer training in prison ministry offered through a criminal justice academy such as suggested above. Candidates on both deacon and elder track
should be required to undergo this training.
- Encourage the Council of Bishops to lead the church in prison
ministry. A good place for the bishops to start is to issue an
episcopal statement on criminal justice and prison ministry
that congregations can use as a study document.
- Urge pastors to address issues of restorative justice from the
pulpit.
- Encourage local congregations and their mission-based organizations (such as United Methodist Men and United
Methodist Women) to study issues related to restorative justice and/or criminal justice matters.
- Become involved in prison ministry in local prisons, jails, and
youth development and youth detention centers and support
prison ministry organizations such as DISCIPLE, Kairos
Prison Ministry International, Epiphany, Yoke Fellows,
MATCH, others through participation and financial support.
- Support the ministry of chaplains in area prisons. Where chaplains are community funded, congregations can provide financial support.
- Support ministry to ex-offenders following release by reaching out to ex-offenders and their families. Support church-
based halfway houses and aftercare initiatives.

Recommendations for United Methodist Seminaries

James M. Shopshire, Sr.

The thirteen United Methodist seminaries are likely to continue
their role of providing formal theological education and equipping
people for ordained ministry in the church. How can the seminaries
and schools of theology strengthen the preparation of restorative justice ministries as part of their work of fulfilling the church's need for
capable and faithful leadership in local churches and in a wide range

of specialized ministry institutions? In this book prison chaplaincy has been our primary focus for ordained leadership. Yet it is one among many other forms of service concerned with healing and restoring vital conditions and relationships in and among persons and communities.

What follows are suggested areas of conversation among the three ministry communities and their immediate connections (the United Methodist Endorsing Agency, the Association of United Methodist Theological Schools, etc.), related general boards and agencies, the Council of Bishops, and annual conference boards of ordained ministry. To be sure, this conversation is already taking place. However, it should be intentionally extended into the next Criminal Justice Summit and the process of evaluating outcomes, planning for change, and implementing new or reorganized initiatives of ministry.

- Engage the Association of United Methodist Theological Schools in an extensive exploration of the needs and issues in restorative justice ministry. Enlarge the view of prospects and problems with chaplaincies (prison ministry in particular), and begin a more intensive consultative process as partners in ministry with the Council of Bishops and the annual conferences.
- Consult and assist the Association of United Methodist Theological Schools in developing curricular approaches to education for specialized ministry, particularly for those who will serve as ministers in prisons and in other institutional settings of criminal justice and prison ministry.
- Identify courses and curricular programs that may be developed specifically for restorative justice ministry and prison ministry. Develop broader courses on a range of justice matters that would include criminal justice issues in the study of religion and society.
- Pinpoint courses and programs that may be offered in modules or special focus on criminal justice and prison ministry. Courses in pastoral care and counseling; personal and social ethics; the family and the faith and action of the church; congregational and

community-based ministry; biblical and theological foundations for justice ministry—all represent possibilities.

- Develop programs and/or courses with ecumenical and interfaith groups, theological consortia, and parachurch organizations that concentrate on preventive ministry prior to incarceration, ministry with persons and families inside and outside of prisons and jails, reentry ministry for formerly incarcerated persons, and ministry with and sometimes prophetic challenge of criminal justice personnel and structures (policy makers, prison administrators, the bench, the bar, parole officers, correctional officers, police, etc.).

- Challenge the seminaries and schools of theology to collaborate in offering educational programs in ministry that can serve the church and are cost-effective. For example, prison ministry curricula could be instituted in three seminaries in the eastern, central, and western United States to serve all the seminaries and the whole denomination. Or a seminary study center could be organized in each of the five jurisdictions to prepare for prison ministry or restorative justice ministry. In either case, the curriculum would be cooperative so that students in any of the seminaries could receive focused theological education for service in prisons, congregations, and communities.

- Sponsor or form partnerships in developing courses and certification programs for clergy and laity in various aspects of prison ministry. The same programs could be designed to equip chaplains and volunteers, candidates for endorsement, and other certifications for service inside prisons and jails and outside with families of victims and offenders. Strategic programs should be designed to reach congregations and community-based organizations for prison ministry, advocacy action groups for reform and change, and community organizing for restorative justice ministry with prison justice systems—local, state, and federal. Programs of this type could pursue the goal of empowering congregations and whole communities to live out of a different understanding of punishment and justice.

- Assist certified local pastors through the Course of Study in preparing for various aspects of prison ministry. Their ministry will bring them in contact with most of the same people and situations that pastors in degree programs face. The Course of Study has an important role to play in providing educational experiences to raise consciousness and equip local pastors and their members for holistic criminal justice ministry.
- Call on the seminaries to develop a systematic process of evaluating outcomes and effectiveness of the *Social Principles* and guidelines set forth for prison and restorative justice ministries in the *Book of Discipline* and the *Book of Resolutions*. Strengthen persons, groups, and programs already engaged in applying these important general church resources and initiatives, and shed more light on resolutions that receive too little attention in prison ministry.
- Educate and engage both laity and clergy on the issues pertaining to the national "race to incarcerate." While criminal justice and prison ministry are about more than racial ethnicity, critical disparities in incarceration and sentencing of Black people, men in particular, and Hispanics/Latinos require urgent attention. The color-blind myth will not suffice while Blacks and Hispanics are arrested, convicted, and incarcerated at much higher rates than their proportion in the population would tolerate in a truly just criminal justice system. In addition, there are fewer prosecutors, judges, and administrators among people of color in the criminal justice system, from the local to the federal level. After acknowledging the reality of racial and ethnic disparities, we need to deal with gender issues and generational issues. It follows that differences in socioeconomic location are important in the work of criminal justice—jails are overcrowded with poor people, not the rich.

Conclusion: Encouragement for the Journey Ahead

Among the many ways that criminal justice ministry can be engaged, The United Methodist Church should advocate for and support practical restorative movements for dealing differently with drug-related felons. The tendency to criminalize lesser crimes in order to rational-ize building more prisons and keeping them full calls forth prophetic advocacy and action for change. Drug courts have been suggested as a means to deal with violators without increasing the recidivist cycle for all-too-many. Increasingly, a contemporary socio-logic that begins with critical social analysis should be used to make Bible study a forum for church members to better understand the Scriptures with reference to the broken places in the lives of people and communities in the here and now of prisons and injustice. Then it would be easier to appre-ciate how our response to God's presence and restorative action can be transformative in the lives of people in prisons as well as churches and communities. Learning how to confront and combat the calculated immoral greed of the prison-industrial complex is another concrete area of ministry to be waged on the local, state, and national levels.

The United Methodist heritage in prison ministry and advocacy for prison reform is an appropriate launching point into criminal justice and prison ministry in the twenty-first century. Ministry to people and systems that have lost sight of their intended purpose in life is not easy. This is the challenge we face within ourselves, our church structures, our nation, and our world.

The quest for restorative justice is a fitting umbrella under which we can extend this important work. We need a socio-logic that allows us as a church to understand the needs, problems, and issues pertaining to holistic justice ministry. We also need a theo-logic that gives guidance along the way. Let it be our proactive prayer that we can face the chal-lenges of criminal justice ministry and work faithfully and effectively as agents of release and restorers of health, justice, and peace.

NOTES

1. *The Book of Resolutions of The United Methodist Church—2004* (Nashville: The United Methodist Publishing House, 2004), 650.
2. Marc Maurer and the Sentencing Project, *Race To Incarcerate* (New York: The New Press, 1999), 193.
3. *Book of Resolutions*, 659–65.

FOR FURTHER READING

Bayse, Daniel J. *Helping Hands: A Handbook for Volunteers in Prison.* Upper Marlboro, MD: American Correctional Association, 1993.

Bureau of Justice Statistics. U.S. Department of Justice, Office of Justice Programs. Available online at *http://www.ojp.usdoj.gov/bjs/*.

Burton-Rose, Daniel, ed., with Dan Pens and Paul Wright. *The Celling of America: An Inside Look at the U.S. Prison Industry.* Monroe, ME: Common Courage Press, 1998.

Costanzo, Mark. *Just Revenge: Costs and Consequences of the Death Penalty.* New York: St. Martin's Press, 1997.

Dammer, Harry R. *Religion in Corrections: Rights and Responsibilities of Inmates, Staff and Volunteers Course.* Lanham, MD: American Correctional Association, 2000.

Davis, Angela. *Are Prisons Obsolete?* New York: Seven Stories Press, 2003.

Elsner, Alan. *Gates of Injustice: The Crisis in America's Prisons.* Upper Saddle River, NJ: Financial Times Prentice Hall, 2004.

Heavner, Betsey. *Congregational Tool Box for Prison Ministry.* Nashville: Discipleship Resources, 2007. Available only as PDF download. See *http://www.discipleshipresources.org*.

Heitzenrater, Richard P., ed. *The Poor and the People Called Methodists, 1729–1999* Nashville: Kingswood, 2002.

Herivel, Tara and Paul Wright, eds. *Prison Nation: The Warehousing of America's Poor.* New York: Routledge, 2003.

Hope Felder, Cain. *Black Men in Prison: The Response of the African American Church*. Atlanta: Interdenominational Center Press, 1990.

Jennings, Jr., Theodore W. *Good News to the Poor: John Wesley's Evangelical Economics*. Nashville: Abingdon, 1990.

Johnstone, Gerry. *Restorative Justice: Ideas, Values, Debates*. Devon, United Kingdom: Willan Publishing, 2002.

Lincoln, C. Eric. *Coming Through the Fire: Surviving Race and Place in America*. Durham, NC: Duke University Press, 1996.

Logan, James Samuel. *Good Punishment? Christian Moral Practice and U.S. Imprisonment*. Grand Rapids, MI: Eerdmans, 2008.

Macquiban, Tim. "Imprisonment and Release in the Writings of the Wesleys," in *Retribution, Repentance, and Reconciliation*. Ed. Kate Cooper and Jeremy Gregory. Woodbridge: Boydell, 2004.

Mauer, Marc and the Sentencing Project. *Race to Incarcerate*. Rev. and updated, 2nd ed. New York: The New Press, 2006.

Mauer, Marc and Meda Chesney-Lind, eds. *Invisible Punishment: The Collateral Consequences of Mass Imprisonment*. New York: The New Press, 2002.

Petersila, Joan. *When Prisoners Come Home: Parole and Prison Reentry*. New York: Oxford University Press, 2003.

Meeks, M. Douglas, ed. *The Portion of the Poor: Good News to the Poor in the Wesleyan Tradition*. Nashville: Kingswood, 1995.

Moyer, Mogene L. *The Changing Roles of Women in the Criminal Justice System*. Prospect Heights, IL: Waveland Press, 1992.

Spitale, Lennie. *Prison Ministry: Understanding Prison Culture Inside and Out*. Nashville: Broadman and Holman, 2002.

Wideman, John Edgar. *Brothers and Keepers*. New York: Houghton Mifflin, 2005.

Wray Harmon L., with Peggy Hutchison, Study Guide by Brenda Connelly. *Restorative Justice: Moving Beyond Punishment*. New York: General Board of Global Ministries, The United Methodist Church, 2002.

Zehr, Howard. *Changing Lenses: A New Focus for Crime and Justice*. Scottdale, PA: Herald Press, 1990.

For Further Reading

The Sentencing Project: Research and Advocacy for Reform (*http://www.sentencingproject.org*) offers excellent resources on a wide variety of issues in criminal justice and prison ministry. Many of these resources are available free of charge under the "Publications" tab on the website. Here are just a few:

- *Selected Bibliography for Advocates on Behalf of Children Prosecuted As Adults* (October 1999).
- King, Ryan S. *The State of Sentencing 2007: Developments in Policy and Practice* (January 2008).
- *Federal Crack Cocaine Sentencing* (January 2008).
- *Facts about Prison and Prisoners* (December 2007).

CONTRIBUTORS

Patricia Barrett is assistant general secretary in the Division of Ordained Ministry, General Board of Higher Education and Ministry, The United Methodist Church, where she is also the endorsing agent for the denomination. She is an elder in the Greater New Jersey Annual Conference of The United Methodist Church.

Richard P. Heitzenrater is William Kellon Quick Professor of Church History and Wesley Studies at the Divinity School, Duke University, Durham, North Carolina. He is an elder in the Western Pennsylvania Annual Conference of The United Methodist Church.

Mark C. Hicks is the Founding Director of Disciple Bible Outreach Ministries of NC, Inc., Jamestown, North Carolina. He is an elder in the Western North Carolina Annual Conference of The United Methodist Church.

Gregory Vaughn Palmer is Presiding Bishop of the Illinois Area of The United Methodist Church and president of the denomination's Council of Bishops.

James M. Shopshire, Sr., is Professor of the Sociology of Religion at Wesley Theological Seminary, Washington, D.C., and an elder in the Iowa Annual Conference of The United Methodist Church.

Richmond Stoglin is a Navy chaplain at Camp LeJeune, North Carolina. He recently retired from the Federal Bureau of Prisons after more than twenty years as prison chaplain. He is an elder in the Mississippi Annual Conference of The United Methodist Church.

Dallas Terrell is Office Assistant to the Pastor in Residence in the Development Office at Gammon Theological Seminary, Interdenominational Theological Center, Atlanta, Georgia.

Janet Wolf is professor and chair of the Division of Church Vocations, American Baptist College, Nashville, Tennessee. She is an elder in the Tennessee Annual Conference of The United Methodist Church.

Josiah U. Young, III, is Professor of Systematic Theology at Wesley Theological Seminary, Washington, D.C. He is an elder in the New York Annual Conference of The United Methodist Church.

Printed in the United States
128842LV00003B/2/P

9 780938 162896